This icon represents the GLORY OF GOD – the eternal value at the centre of the Christian faith. The Greek Fathers called it the *perichoresis (peri:* around, *chora:* place), the dance of love of the Trinity in which they give place to each other. This is the glory revealed in Jesus, as the Father and the Son give authority to each other in mutual interdependence, and as the creator and the creation interpenetrate each other. Both God's love and human nature realize their perfection in a new creation which is the marriage of heaven and earth.

To Sandra, my dancing partner

Other books by Stephen Verney

Fire in Coventry
People and Cities
Into the New Age
Water into Wine

A Letter to the Reader

Stephen died suddenly in November 2009 and, since then people from everywhere have been asking me where they might find copies of his books.

In 2010, Fire in Coventry, his first book was beautifully reintroduced by Bishop Christopher Cocksworth. Then, in 2012, Janet Wagon, our great friend and neighbour unearthed an old, fragmented typescript of The Dance of Love, Stephen's fifth book. Somehow she revived it and brought it into the digital age. My task was to edit each chapter as it arrived and store it on the Cloud, where, no doubt, Stephen did a double check. Eventually, The Dance of Love was re-born.

I would like to thank everyone in England, Wales and USA for weeping and laughing with me over each 'new' chapter and for pushing me forward whenever I faltered.

Most of all, I want to thank Stephen, who led me on to the dance floor, and danced with me for twenty nine years.

Sandra Verney
Blewbury, Oxfordshire

STEPHEN VERNEY

❖❖

The Dance of Love

First published in Great Britain by
Fount Paperbacks, London in 1989

Copyright © 1989 by Stephen Verney

This edition published in 2013 by Verney Books

ISBN 978-0-9926856-0-7

CONTENTS

FOREWORD

I was walking the Ridgeway recently, that ancient path used by our ancestors from prehistoric times, which runs along the Berkshire Downs behind the village of Blewbury where I now live. I was walking with my god-daughter, Zoe, and we found to our great convenience and pleasure that there were excellent signposts pointing the way. But imagine that you were lost up there in a fog, and that when by good luck you stumbled upon a signpost, somebody had twisted it round to point in the wrong direction!

That is what has happened with our key Christian words, such as "glory", "repentance", "forgiveness". They are signposts pointing us the way home, but they have got twisted round, and in the popular language of today they no longer have their original significance. I call them key words because they fit the locks in our human nature. They are beautifully designed, to fit those locks very precisely and to open the doors. But if our keys have got bent, and our doors are locked, then we cannot get in or out; there might be a fire in your house and you and your family could not get out, or you might arrive home after a long journey and you could not get in.

A crisis such as that has in fact arrived. We are living at a moment of great danger and great opportunity, in which we urgently need to return to the traditional truth of Christ, and to rediscover his words in the context of today – in the context of Chernobyl and AIDS, but also of an emerging partnership between men and women and a new understanding of the nature of the physical universe. His truth can save the world, and not just our own souls; but we encounter a deep frustration, because the key words in which we have to proclaim that traditional truth no longer resonate in our minds and hearts with their original meaning. They no longer fit the locks and open the doors, either that door inside each one of us to the secret centre in the depth of ourselves where we meet God, or the doors between us so that we can listen to the anguish and the joy in the depth of each other, and recognize that we are one. When we use the words – and there are no other words to use – they call up images which are often diametrically opposed to their true meaning. For example if we proclaim repentance, what people hear and quite rightly reject is a command to grovel like a guilty worm before an almighty and angry dictator. They do not hear a call to new relationships.

Why should this be? The cause lies partly in our materialistic culture, for people who have become obsessed with money and power no longer ask the questions to which these words provide the answer – questions about our relations with nature, with each other and with God, or the profound question "who am I?". Isaiah, in his day, was confronted by the same impasse, and he wrote with a bitter irony:

> Make the hearts of this people dull,
> And their ears heavy,
> And shut their eyes
> Lest they see with their eyes,
> And hear with their ears,
> And understand with their hearts,
> And return and be healed.

But partly the cause lies deeper within ourselves, and it is the same in every culture. For these words are signposts pointing us into the mystery of God – into "the cloud of unknowing". They are guiding us towards a reality which cannot be grasped by the mind, but which must be known in the heart. As we hear them spoken, our ears cannot hear their true meaning. Jesus himself was confronted by this very same impasse, and acknowledged it when he said "He that has ears to hear let him hear"; and when he told his listeners, "you can only know this truth as you do it".

Before we can proclaim the traditional truth of Christ to our generation, so that they may "return and be healed", we must first return to those healing words within ourselves; they have grown stale, like yesterday's bread, and we must rediscover them coming fresh out of our own experience. Then we must remind each other, with fear and trembling, that we can only know in our hearts the truth those words express as we do that truth together.

I offer this book to anyone who would like to come with me on such a journey of rediscovery. Here is our itinerary.

The book is written in three parts. First, we return to 9 key Christian words – there are of course many other words we might have chosen, such as "faith" and "salvation", but they would fill many books. Secondly, we go on an outer journey into the materialistic culture of our day, and an inner journey into the mystery of the presence of God. I hope you will be as surprised and excited as I am to discover that the living truth we are searching for is coming to meet us out of the very materialism, and out of the very mystery, which seemed to be blocking it off. Then, thirdly, we return to the origin and to the focus of Christian truth, to Jesus in his crucifixion and resurrection, and having become a little clearer about what some of the key words mean, we expose ourselves to the Word itself, to hear it and receive it. Finally, in a brief conclusion, I make some suggestions about doing the truth which we have heard.

The different parts of the book have come together from different sources. The discussion of key words comes from articles I wrote for the magazine "Christian", encouraged by its editor, Charles Elliott. "The Spirit of the Age" comes from a talk I gave at a conference of the Guild of Pastoral Psychology, and "Images of God in Prayer" from a lecture in Chelmsford Cathedral. I am grateful to the Guild, and to John Moses, the Provost of Chelmsford, for giving me these opportunities, and prodding me into this activity. "Seeing the wood for the Trees" grows out of a lifelong study of St John's gospel. But though they began in different places, all these parts have ended up in a unity, and all the strands are woven together into one book. I have been continually conscious, as I wrote, that a truth greater than I could grasp was actively moulding all these pieces together, and seeking, through my unknowing, to make itself known. I owe most of the ideas in this book to other people, whom I have worked with and suffered with or perhaps met casually on a train! In particular, I am grateful to Fred Blum, with whom I have travelled for 20 years, and whose ideas are woven in and out of my own.

I have especially to thank my neighbour, Janet Wagon, for taking my rough copy and transforming it into a beautiful typescript on her word processor, and for keeping calm when I got agitated.

Above all I have to thank Sandra, my wife, who for weeks on end put up with my total selfishness as I wrote this book about love.

Stephen Verney

I
WORDS

‍

1

Glory: The dance of love

Like Moses we say to God, "Please, show me your glory."

We return first to the word glory not only because glory is the beginning from which we come and the end towards which we go, but because it is only the vision of glory which has the power to transform us, and to create that "paradigm shift" which will enable the human race to survive.

The word in Hebrew is *kabod*, meaning literally the weight or value of a thing. If you go to the greengrocer to buy a cauliflower, he will weigh it on his scales and tell you how much it is worth. The glory of God is God's weight or worth; and so it comes to mean his character, what he really is, which shines out of him so that we can see it. When we see it we worship him, or declare his worth, or glorify him.

Nobody can paint God's portrait, but the Orthodox church have an icon, reproduced inside the front cover of this book, of the three angels who came to visit Abraham, and to bring him the promise of a son. They are seated round a table, and their three figures are related to each other, motionless, but in a graceful dance, in the giving and receiving of love. One looks at the other, and that second looks at the third, whose eyes are turned inwards into the mystery of the self. Through that dance of love there is revealed to us the glory of God. Through that unity which is diversity, and that diversity which is unity, there dawns upon us the mystery of God's name, which is I AM.

That glory, that I AM, which cannot be defined or grasped by the human mind, is focused in Jesus. In him we see the dance of love. The most accurate and penetrating description of that dance is given us in St John's gospel, chapter five. The religious authorities have accused Jesus of making himself equal to God, and he replies in words which move beyond the category of equality, and into the language of love. "The Son can do nothing of himself", he says, "but only what he sees the Father doing" (v.19). That is one side of the equation (of this so-called equality) – the emptiness of the Son. He looks, and what he sees the Father doing, that he does; he listens, and what he hears the Father saying, that he says. The other side of the equation – of the choreography – is the generosity of the Father. "The Father loves the Son, and reveals to him everything which he is doing" (v.20), and furthermore, he gives him authority to do "out of himself" all that the Father does, and can never cease to do because it flows "out of himself". In that dance of love between them, says Jesus, "I and the Father are one." The Son cries "Abba! Father!" and the Father cries "my beloved Son", and the love which leaps between them is Holy Spirit – the Spirit of God, God himself, for God is Spirit and God is Love. The Spirit is the third in the dance – as the music itself is the third when Geraint Evans is singing an aria from Mozart's Don Giovanni; then there are three, the singer, the song, and the music sounding, now, in the opera house and being heard by the audience. So God, in that dance of love, knows himself in the eternal now, and says I AM.

The dance of love is the glory in God's heart, but is also the pattern which is reflected in everything he has created. We experience it as the inmost truth of I AM in ourselves – in the marriage between sexuality and spirituality in each one of us. But most clearly it is reflected in the marriage of male and female. "Male and female created he them. In the image of God created he them." Each of us can come to know the masculine and the feminine dancing together in ourselves, but it is the to and fro of human love between husband and wife, their confrontation, their commitment to each other over a lifetime "till death us do part", which allows the pattern of eternity to be acted out most naturally in time. At the heart of human marriage is the mystery of two persons becoming one flesh, of differentiation and unity, of vulnerability and forgiveness; and day by day the rediscovery of who I AM, and of the "hope of glory" realized, as we come home to each other in the deepening experience of the dance of love.

But this glory is not only revealed in human terms. It is written into all nature. I see it every day in the vegetables growing in my garden, carrots and cabbages, broad beans, dwarf beans and runner beans, leeks and purple sprouting broccoli – each one declaring the glory of God by being itself, but all declaring it together by their variety, and by their interdependence with rain, soil and sun. "O all ye works of the Lord, bless ye the Lord, praise him and magnify him for ever." God is singing through them the song of his glory. But I ask myself, what about the rabbits, the greenfly, the wire-worms and the slugs which eat my vegetables? Are they part of this same concert? Then I remember that the word concert means literally "struggling together", and I recognize that God's music includes and holds together many dissonances.

Similarly, his glory is written into human history interwoven with suffering. One of the significant factors in the history of our own twentieth century is the modern city, that complex whole where many problems and much suffering meet – pollution, homelessness, unemployment, violence. But in that very complexity we become aware of the glory: that we are interdependent, we belong to each other, and that the city will work for us and become an opportunity as we learn to obey the command "love one another". In Liverpool during the 1980s which some outsiders saw as a city of riots and litter in the streets, but where insiders said, "I wouldn't live anywhere else", the Roman Catholic Archbishop and the Anglican Bishop, as it were, led the dance together, and invited everybody to join in. This is more influential than any number of sermons, because it points us towards the vision of glory which alone has power to transform our human egocentricity, and to bring us to a new way of seeing things which makes possible a new way of doing things.

"To him be glory in the church", wrote St Paul. The church is essentially a diversity in unity, the body with many limbs and organs, the fellowship of the Holy Spirit. Why then are we at loggerheads? Why have we tortured each other with unspeakable savagery, and burnt each other at the stake? Why are there such fierce tensions inside religious communities, and within parishes? Is it because we are called, by the very character and glory of God, not into a static truth but into a dance – into the acceptance and expression of our differences around the still centre which is himself, into listening to each other, and letting each other go? Does the glory lie not in being right, but in forgiveness? For the last two years I have been meeting with Orthodox, Roman Catholic and Anglican men and women, to identify the issues which underlie the ordination of women, and to expose ourselves to the mysteries of masculine/feminine and of priesthood which we cannot fully grasp with the human mind because God is in them. Listening to each other, and being vulnerable, we have glimpsed something of a glory which might be drawing us all together towards a deeper truth, which none of us have so far understood or expressed in our ecclesiastical structures. But at that point, the structures themselves react in alarm. They say "Stop!" and the glory is overcome by the power of darkness.

I saw the same thing happening four years ago in the coal strike. A number of us, including representatives from the Coal Board and the National Union of Mineworkers, sat together secretly and listened to each other. We became vulnerable, and gradually over some weeks we opened up the pain which was in our hearts – the son of a pit manager was on strike, and the son of a union official had gone back to work. Looking back, I can see now that something of the glory was in that room, transforming us, so that as we learnt to trust each other we "resolved" the strike. Then we took our solution out into the structures of power, both government and trade union, and it was rejected. Again, looking back, I can see that glory has to come face to face with evil, and to fail and to suffer and to die.

We can only see the glory as we look back. When Moses said to God, "Please, show me your glory", God replied, "You cannot see my face, for no man shall see me and live . . . So it shall be, while my glory passes by, that I will put you in the cleft of the rock, and will cover you with my hand while I pass by. Then I will take away my hand and you shall see my back; but my face shall not be seen."

So it is as we remember that supreme event, when the glory of God is focused in the crucifixion of Jesus. Here is the dance of love. Here Jesus prays, "Glorify your son, that your Son may glorify you". Here the Son is most empty and most vulnerable, and here the Father gives him the ultimate authority to save the world. Here the structures of religion and of the state reject the glory, and the glory comes face to face with darkness and with evil, and fails and suffers and dies. We cannot grasp the meaning of that crucifixion with our minds, nor even with our imaginations, and if we looked into the face of that glory we would die. But as we look back and remember, the risen Jesus comes to meet us out of the eternal depths of each present moment, and out of the secret centre of ourselves, and invites us to join the dance.

Let the poets speak for us. T. S. Eliot wrote, for our generation:

> At the still point of the turning world
> There the dance is.

And Lewis Carroll wrote, in a nonsense poem for a child in Wonderland:

> Turn not pale beloved snail,
> But come and join the dance.

2

Repentance: A change of mind and heart

Now we come to that key word in the proclamation of Jesus which opens the door to glory. On Easter Day Jesus sent his disciples to every nation and culture to proclaim ... what? Very few Christians know the answer, although it is printed in our bibles. I have put this question to many groups of Christians, including a House of Bishops, in UK, Canada, USA, Australia, Germany. Not one in a hundred could remember what Jesus actually said. Why not?

For two reasons. First because our English word, *repentance*, does not carry the true meaning of what he said. In New Testament Greek the word is *metanoia*, which means a change of mind and heart. (*meta* = change *noia* = the whole mind, intellect, feeling, desire and will). The English word repentance comes from a different root altogether, from the Greek word *poine* which means punishment. *Poine* was the name of the Goddess of Vengeance, who exacted blood money as a ransom which set you free from the consequences of committing murder. So the word *repentance* in English positively misleads us. We sense quite rightly that Jesus cannot be commanding us to feel guilty and plead guilty before the God of Vengeance. This cannot be his Good News. So when we tune in to that first Easter day, and try to remember what Jesus said, the word repentance does not come up on the screen of our memory.

The second reason we do not remember is that *metanoia* points to something terrifying and beyond our comprehension. We are being commanded by Jesus to let go what we thought we knew. *Metanoia* is a return home to something profoundly old and a discovery that it is something radically new – our eyes are to be opened to see everything differently, and our desire is to be transformed – we are to be no longer individuals in control of our own lives, but to enter into the dance of love with God and with each other.

This command to *metanoia* challenges our whole *zeitgeist* – our individualism and our materialism. It calls us to change our idea of ourselves, and our scientific view of the universe. I will explore these ideas later (see pages 65–69).

But the most profound challenge of *metanoia* is to our idea of God. A Catholic Council which met recently in Rome reported that five years ago they had seen the enemy as materialism, but that now they recognized an equal danger in religious fundamentalism. These two, materialism and religious fundamentalism, appear in their own eyes to be opposites, but we may suspect that they represent the two polarities of an outdated world view which is now breaking apart – a material world and an isolated immutable God, locked together in an unholy struggle. True *metanoia* involves letting go not only of materialism but also of our idea of God, for he is a mystery beyond our comprehension, and to cling to what we think we know about him is to make the fundamental error.

The *metanoia* which Jesus commands us to proclaim to all nations is that with him we are born again into a new creation, where God and human nature are in dialogue, and each of us can discover the truth of what I AM in that dance of Love. Jesus does not define *metanoia* but he tells stories about it. One of these stories he told to the religious fundamentalists of his own day.

A man had one hundred sheep, and lost one of them. Instead of following the shepherd it had chosen another path, and now night was falling and the wolves were lurking in the hills ready to tear it in pieces. There was nothing it could do but bleat. But the shepherd was searching for it. He left the *ninety-nine*, and searched for the one until he found it. Then in this little story the word joy appears three times. He laid the sheep on his shoulders rejoicing, and carried it home. He called his friends and neighbours, and said "Rejoice with me". Then Jesus says something which turns our world upside down. "There is more joy in heaven over one sinner who repents than over *ninety-nine* righteous people who have no need of repentance."

Here we learn three truths which make up the pattern of *metanoia*.

We are lost: We have chosen our own path, and now we are imprisoned in our ego-centricity, and in the evil of the world around us.

God is searching for us: In our spiritual journey, which seems at first to be our search for God, there has to come this radical switch of understanding – that out of the depths of each present moment, out of everything that happens, out of our own bellies, God the Spirit and the energy of Love is searching for us and finding us.

Then there is joy: Joy in my own heart, because what I most desire has come to me – the dance of Love between heaven and earth is breaking out of the innermost centre of myself. Joy to the world, because in our powerlessness we are being given to each other. Joy in the heart of God; and because God is everywhere, then as one human being enters into the dance of Love with him, joy reverberates through the whole universe, through every galaxy and rock and earthworm, and through every human culture now and throughout all time. Then there is more joy in heaven and on earth than over the *ninety-nine* righteous who have no need of *metanoia*, because they think they already know God. Being blind they think they see, so they do not ask for and receive his free gift.

Metanoia is the change from I to I AM. "I" is my ego-centric self, my twilight self, grasping, trying to control and manipulate, seeking wealth, power and reputation. I AM is my true self, which has become aware of the presence of God springing up from within my human personality. To receive the free gift of *metanoia* is to receive the mind and heart of Jesus, who said of himself I AM. He was affirming the whole of his human nature, and in the same present moment recognizing within himself the name of God. The heart of the consciousness of Jesus is "I and the Father who sent me". It is that dance of Love between Father and Son, in which "the Son can do nothing of himself", but the Father gives him authority to raise the dead and recreate the universe.

When I was a schoolboy of seventeen I visited Greece, and walked into the church at Daphne. There in the dome over my head was a face of Christ such as I had never seen in my life before. He was terrifying in his majesty and his love. His hand was raised in blessing, and in it I saw the print of the nail. In every Orthodox Church there is such an icon of Christ Pantokrator ("The Ruler of all things") seated in glory, and it expresses the ultimate vision of *metanoia*. It is a new way of seeing God and the whole universe and ourselves. At the centre of the New Creation is Jesus the Christ. In him is the marriage of heaven and earth, and he has opened the possibility of it for us. He, the good shepherd, has become the lost sheep, and by his compassion he has opened the eyes of the blind, he has set free prisoners, and he has called the dead out of their tombs. Now the whole universe is gathered around him, into a "field", where everything in heaven and on earth cries in adoration "Jesus Christ is Lord"; where everything has meaning, and everything belongs together, and together they sing the song of God's glory.

3

❧

Forgiveness: Letting go

I remember once in India meeting with a Hindu scholar.
After I had asked him about Hinduism he began asking me
about Christianity, and the greatest puzzle to him was this
word forgiveness. "It appears that you have an account
book", he said, "with debts written on one side. You are
suggesting that God simply crosses out the debts. That
seems to me unrealistic and immoral."

I meet with many people in this country who call themselves lapsed Christians, to whom this word forgiveness is
also a puzzle. It conjures up a picture of a judge leaning
over the ramparts of heaven and saying: "You are a wicked,
vicious man (or woman). Because you have grovelled before
me and pleaded guilty, I am prepared to overlook it this
time. But don't do it again." Quite rightly they have rejected
such a religion, or "lapsed" from it.

What does the word forgiveness mean? It is like a plant
with a deep and complex root system, but I want to concen-
trate on the flower which emerges in the New Testament,
and which becomes a central theme in the Lord's Prayer,
"Forgive us ... as we forgive". When we read the word
forgiveness in the New Testament it is in the huge majority
of cases a translation of the Greek word *aphesis*, and
aphesis means letting go.

When I look the word up in a Greek Lexicon I find that it
means letting go prisoners, or ransoming slaves. It has also
the sense of letting go or relaxing tension: for example, if a
rope is stretched and taut, and you let it go, that is *aphesis*.
There is another intriguing use of the word – *aphesis* is the
name given to the starting line on a race course. We may

imagine horses lined up for a race such as the Grand National, reined in by their jockeys. The steward says "Go!", and the horses go galloping off along the course. He has "let them go", to be and do what they have it in them to be and do, – beautiful horses galloping and leaping over hurdles.

This word *aphesis*, letting go, expresses very accurately what Jesus himself said he had come to do, and which he describes in a variety of colourful images. For example, he has come to set free prisoners out of prison.

On a Good Friday recently I was in a prison, and 30 prisoners came to a discussion group about the crucifixion of Jesus. "What does it mean", I asked them, "that Jesus came to set free prisoners?" Then they began to tell me. "The real prison is not this one we are sitting in", they said. One of them quoted:

> Stone walls do not a prison make
> Nor iron bars a cage.

"The real prison is in here", said another, pointing into himself. "The prison is fear", said a third. They told me of the terrible fear of being in your cell, and then being led up into the court, where the judge looks at you, and you are totally exposed, and he condemns you, and the whole world falls about your ears. Then others began to describe their experience in prison – how they had come to know Jesus as another kind of judge who stands beside you in compassion, reveals yourself to yourself, and sets you free – how they had come to hear his words in a new sense – how when everybody has been found out and you are all at the bottom of the pile together, you can share the meaning of those words with each other. One of them said, "By coming to prison I have been set free." "Do you really mean that?", I asked him. "Yes", he said. "It's a horrible experience, but in a way it has been a privilege."

18

Forgiveness: Letting go

Jesus said that he had come to set free prisoners, or using another image, to call the dead out of their tombs. As we began to see in the last two chapters, looking into the words "glory" and "repentance", the real tomb in which we lie dead is not in some cemetery or other. Like my friend in the prison, we have to point into ourselves. The tomb is "I". Dead is "not knowing God". Jesus calls us out of "I" and into I AM, which is to know God in the dance of Love, and to experience his Spirit in the to and fro of Love with each other. When Jesus called Lazarus out of the tomb he called upon the people standing round to share in the work of *aphesis*. "Loose him", he said, "and let him go"; the words have the sense "let him go on his way to God", like a horse galloping off along the race course towards the winning post.

It is profoundly moving and revealing that when Jesus was himself a prisoner, and actually being put to death, he prayed "Father, let them go." They were the real prisoners – Pilate, Caiaphas and the rest. They were the real corpses in the tomb. What he was achieving through his crucifixion was to open the prison door and roll away the stone from the tomb, and to "let them go."

That is what he did, but how did he achieve it? I caught a glimpse of the "how" one evening in a l'Arche home for mentally handicapped people, where I heard Doris, one of the handicapped ladies, cry out of the agony in her heart that she had been rejected by her own family and put into an institution. The next morning one of the assistants, who were living in this home with their mentally handicapped brothers and sisters, told me how that cry had pierced through her defences, and through the protective screens she had built round herself, and penetrated right into her heart. "I came to realise last night", she said, "that I too felt rejected. I have never dared face it before, but I knew that Doris was facing it with me. Now, this morning, for the first time in my life, I feel that I can be loved."

Notice that she did not say "now I can love", but "now I can be loved." The prison in which she had been a prisoner all her life was the "I" who was afraid to be loved, because it would be too dangerous and painful. But that evening the cry of Doris resonated inside her own experience, and compassion unlocked the door – for compassion means "suffering together". That is how Jesus unlocks the prison door and lets us go. He is with us, in compassion, at the very heart and centre of our fear.

But though his compassion opens the prison door, we ourselves have to choose to step out into our own freedom. The *aphesis* he offers is sometimes said to be "unconditional forgiveness", but this is not true. There is a very clear condition laid down. Being set free involves letting go. You will be set free as you let others go.

To be set free absolutely, we have to let go everything. To begin with, we have to let go possessions – to stop clinging to them, because we are the prisoner of what we cling to. For example, as you read this you may be sitting on a chair. If you cling to the chair you are a prisoner of the chair. You can only move a very little way in any direction. But if you let go the chair you can get up and walk about. Then you are a free human being, and the chair is a free chair on which you can rest when necessary.

Similarly, we have to let go people. Parents have to let go their children, when the time is ripe, and children their parents, so that all of them may be free. Husbands have to let go their wives, and wives their husbands – to respect each other, and to encourage each other to grow into the real person which each one potentially is. This letting go is not dropping each other, or opting out. At the profoundest level it is to stop clinging, and to hand each other over into the Love of God.

More difficult for religious people, but this is clearly what Jesus taught, is to let go religion. Do not cling to it, and use it for your own ends, for this is the ultimate sin –

the spiritual pride or blasphemy against the Holy Spirit, for which there is no *aphesis*. So I find myself saying to my Evangelical friends, "Let go the bible. Don't cling to it, and hit people over the head with all those texts. Let it go, so that the Word may enter into you, and take possession of you, and reveal its mystery in you, and flow through you." Similarly I find myself saying to my Catholic friends, "Let go the Eucharist. Don't cling to it, as though it were yours. Let it go, so that it may become the sacrifice of Christ in you – so that you who break the bread may become the bread which God breaks." To myself and others like me, who talk about the Christian life as a journey, I say, "For God's sake arrive!". To us all, "Let go religion, so that we may receive back eternal life."

Then, finally, we have to let go other people's sins. The word is again *aphesis*.

What can it mean – to let go another person's sin First, obviously, that I should not cling to it. If a man or woman is, for example a sadist, or sexually promiscuous, I should not cling to that sin, and secretly enjoy it or outwardly punish it, because this ministers to some secret desire in myself or to some need to punish myself. Secondly, I am told by the risen Jesus to "let go" that person's sin – to let it go galloping along the course like a race horse. This does not mean "let sin rip". But it does mean "recognize it", because that desire which consumes you – your sadism, your sexual promiscuity – points to the deepest and all-consuming desire of your true Self, which is to be loved and to love. Your true Self is locked up in the prison of your ego. The I AM is locked up within the I. So recognize the sin and the energy within it, then in the name of Jesus, in the power of his compassion, and the glory of his new creation, LET IT GO to be expressed and transformed and joyfully experienced in the to and fro of Love between your Self and God, and between you and other people.

4

꞉꞊§꞊꞉

Sin: Missing the mark

We come now to the fourth word – SIN – which means, precisely, that we fall short of Glory.

Sin is a powerful word, a key beautifully designed and accurately cut to turn the stubborn and complex lock in the heart of our human nature. Most damagingly to our health and happiness it is generally misunderstood, so that we speak of people "living in sin" as though the word sin meant sex outside marriage. But the basic meaning of "to sin" is "to miss the mark", as when an archer shoots an arrow which misses the target.

When I was a boy I enjoyed miniature rifle shooting, and I remember a proud day when I scored a "possible" – five bulls eyes in the centre of the target, each shot scoring 10, 50 out of 50. When we sin we miss the target, but what is the target we miss? St Paul defines it very accurately, "all have sinned and come short of the glory of God." The target is Glory – the dance of love between God and our human nature. That is the "possible", but we have all fallen short of it. An occasional shot may hit the nine or the eight or the seven, but most of the time we are off target altogether.

"I am a sinner", means "I miss the target for which I was created", and this missing the mark has two aspects.

First, I am failing to be my true self. I walk about the world not knowing God's love. Sin is a kind of blindness. I do not recognize God in the trees and the rain and the sunshine – I am not aware of God in other people – I do not meet God in the centre of my own being. I may never have committed a murder, or shoplifted, but I am failing to be my

true self, to realize my potential (my "possible"), and to
enter into the dance of Love with nature and with other
people and with God which is true happiness.

Secondly, there is a more serious aspect to this failure. I
choose it. In that secret place in the very centre of my own
being I choose my isolated little ego-self, rather than the
glory of God which is the to and fro of love. I am not altogether to blame for this because I have been brought up in a
society where everybody else is out for themselves. As an
accountant said to me recently, "When you are buying or
selling a house trust nobody, and believe nothing anybody
says to you." Growing up in this society I have been deeply
wounded, and have built round me a protective screen.

Also, I have inherited "self consciousness", which is the
glory of homo sapiens, raising us to a new level of consciousness above that of the vegetables and the animals. This makes
me able to think rationally and to love, to choose and to make
jokes. It makes me feel (not altogether erroneously) that I am
myself the centre of the universe, and that I should fight for
my own survival, and be afraid of what threatens me and try to
control it. So I choose my own glory rather than the glory of
God. This is called original sin.

There are two Jewish-Christian myths which explore the
mystery of original sin. The first is the story of Satan. He
was an archangel and his name was Lucifer, the "light
bearer". He stood very close to the glory of God, and was
privileged to carry something of that light within himself.
He was the servant of God, whose functions was to carry
that light into the affairs of humankind and to "bring to
light" what is in us, in order both to test us and to help us
discriminate between good and evil. But Satan put himself
in God's place. This is the original sin – spiritual pride –
which caused him to rebel against the source of that light
which he had been privileged to carry, and to claim it as his
own. He was cast out of heaven, or perhaps we should say

that by his spiritual pride he cast himself out of heaven, and became the source of temptation and spiritual pride in us.

The second story is about Adam and Eve and the serpent, and it shows us the same original sin latent within ourselves, and unfolding in the development of our human nature. Adam and Eve are living in harmony with God and with nature and with each other. Then the serpent says, "Rise to a new level of self-consciousness, and be like gods, knowing good and evil in yourselves." We call this "the fall", but as William Temple pointed out, in one sense it is a fall upwards – it is an evolution of consciousness, and Lucifer the light bearer is calling Adam and Eve to the destiny which God has prepared for those who love him – to internalise his truth which is "out there" and to let it be "in here". But at the same time he is tempting them to ego-centricity and spiritual pride. "You shall be like gods."

This is the paradox at the heart of our human nature, that as we evolve towards God we rebel against God. It seems that like the prodigal son I have to make a mess of my life in order to "come to myself", and to leave home in order to return home. I am invited by God to "know God", but I have first to let go what I think I "know about God". I am invited in some mysterious way to be one with God, but I have first to lose my ego-self, and in a terrible emptiness to receive back that True Self which is able to be one with God and with nature and with other people in the dance of Love.

The closer a human being comes to know God, the more ferocious is the temptation to spiritual pride. Jesus himself experienced it after his baptism, when the veil between heaven and earth had been torn open, and the Spirit had come upon him, and he had heard the voice saying, "You are my beloved son." Immediately, we read, he was driven into the desert by that very same Spirit which he had just received, to be tempted by Satan. "If you are the beloved Son", said the tempter, "then use your spiritual power to further your cause, which is after all God's cause."

If original sin is spiritual pride, then we have to recognize that the greatest sinners are religious people. "Do not point at the publicans (the dishonest financiers) and the prostitutes", said Jesus, "It is you, not they, who are really living in sin. They may be sinners in the first and less serious sense, that they are failing to be their true selves. But look into yourselves. You are sinners in the far more destructive and poisonous sense that you rebel against God, like Lucifer. God has chosen you to carry his light for others, but you have chosen to make little gods out of yourselves. Your sin is a breach of that fundamental covenant of the to and fro of Love between your human nature and God. It is the deepest kind of adultery and dishonesty".

So who are the greatest sinners in the world today? I would have to reply, "those who appear to be most religious". First, those fundamentalists and traditionalists, men and women of all faiths, who will not let go what they think they know about God. Secondly, those "new age" people and charismatics who have not faced up to the original sin of their own ego-centricity, and who fall into the very temptation which Jesus resisted – putting the True Self into the place of God and not recognizing that I AM is a gift of God to be received afresh every day. I look into my own heart and tremble, because I find these twin sins in myself.

Because the root of sin is spiritual pride we religious people, to be on target again, have to stop taking ourselves so seriously. We have to stop congratulating ourselves that we are spiritual people, and stop thanking God, like the Pharisee in the parable, "that I am not as other men are". We have to relax, and be ordinary, and become more human, for we need more human nature not less if we are to return out of sin into glory. Above all we have to let go of God – to stop clinging to God, trying to monopolize and manipulate him.

The seven deadly sins are pride, jealousy, anger, sloth,

Sin: Missing the mark

avarice, gluttony, lust. Dante lists them in that order, with
pride as the most deadly, and lust the least deadly. They are
seven facets of human nature given us by God to reflect his
own character, but in which we have missed the mark, and
fallen short of glory, by harnessing them to our ego-centricity. When Jesus transforms water into wine, he says, "fill
the water pots with water" – you need more human nature
not less – the whole of your potential offered to God, and
then poured out and given to others. This is the pattern he
demonstrated once for all, when he took the cup, gave
thanks, and gave it to his friends to drink. "This is my life
blood", he said, "the new covenant of the dance of Love
between God and humankind, poured out for you *for the
forgiveness of your sins*" – to let you go free, to let those
seven deadly sins go on their way towards God like seven
arrows flying towards the centre of the target. 70 out of 70!
A "possible"! Human nature caught up into glory.

27

5

❖❖

Grace: The free gift

Trying to rediscover the original meaning of some key Christian words we began with Glory, the word signifying the Dance of love within the very being of the Godhead, which we human beings are created to dance with the Godhead. Ne desire more than anything else on earth to experience hat Glory – to love and to be loved! The two great drives within us, sexuality and spirituality, are searching for Glory but they can never grasp it. It can only be received as a free gift, by GRACE.

The word Grace means, literally, a free gift which there is absolutely no obligation to give. A gift made out of pure good will. A kindness which gives pleasure. The English word grace comes from the Latin *gratis,* and an interesting feature of that Latin word is that in the singular it means grace, or free gift, whereas in the plural *(gratiae)* it means thanks or gratitude. So the very word opens up a dance of love between the giver and the one who receives the gift. Grace leads to gratitude, one free gift works a whole stream of free gifts, and this dance of love is discovered to be the very essence of the Christian life, in which human beings respond with thanksgiving to the free gift of God. In Greek the word is *charis,* meaning grace, loveliness, glory, gratitude, from which come the English words "charisma" (graciousness, attractiveness), and "Eucharist", the giving of thanks (Eucharist means literally "thanking well"). So again we can say that the very essence of the Christian life is God's attractiveness drawing out of us a response of thanksgiving. Grace is a free gift, like a birthday present or

29

a Christmas present, and as we unwrap this present we discover to our astonishment that it is the gift of GLORY. God is giving us the essence of himself, the to and fro of love. What we most desire, what we would spend everything to get, what we have neither earned nor deserved, we are being invited to receive as an absolutely free gift. But it comes to us on two conditions, first that we shall choose it with our own free will and persist in choosing it over the years, and secondly that we shall let it overflow in a to and fro of love with other people – grace overflowing in gratitude.

Now comes the awful self-discovery which seems to dash the cup from our lips. We cannot choose what we most want. As St Paul experienced it, "The good that I will to do I do not do; but the evil I will not to do, that I practice". Our egocentric human nature is not capable of choosing and receiving the free gift of glory.

Grace overcomes this apparent impotence. It reveals itself to be a two-fold gift, both a Christmas present and a birthday present. The first gift is the birthday present. God creates within us and gives us on our birthday an inner chamber as a secret centre within our human nature where we can meet him. Nobody can enter into that secret room except God and ourselves. There, in absolute privacy, we can know him. We can expose our deepest needs and hopes to him, and he can be present to us in his steadfast mercy, and in his love which is beyond words and which cannot be grasped by the mind or even by the imagination. There we can let go both our sexuality and our spirituality, we can let go even our name, so that in our nakedness and emptiness God may reveal to us our true name which can be known only to him and to us. There we can run to meet him, no longer knowing anything about him or about ourselves, to learn his name in the dance of love. This is the first gift of Grace, that God has designed us and created us capable of loving him, capable of sharing his nature, capable of being transformed out of egocentricity and into glory. That is our birthday present.

The second gift of Grace is the Christmas present, that he comes to open the door of our prison, to transform us, to raise us out of the death of not knowing him, and to give us to each other. In Jesus he came to open the secret centre within the human nature of each one of us, so that in our emptiness and unknowing we might become one with him and with each other.

"If you knew the free gift of God," said Jesus. He was talking to a woman of Samaria, beside the deep well of Jacob. He had been sitting there alone, tired from his journey and thirsty from the heat of the day, and looking at the well he had seen how a fountain of flowing water sprang out of the depths of that well shaft. Contemplating that well, he had come to recognize the truth of it in himself – that he *was* such a deep well, and that out of the secret depths of himself there flowed the spring of the presence of God, the glory of God, the to and fro of love. Then the woman had arrived, and he saw that she too had it in her to be such a well. Out of the secret centre of herself, out of the reality of her human nature, there could flow the glory of God, but only if she fulfilled the two conditions for receiving the free gift. She would have to make an act of choice – she would have to ask for it. Then she would have to share it, because you cannot live the to and fro of love unless it actually passes to and fro between you and somebody else. So first, between herself and Jesus. "Give me water," he says to her. "I ask you for water, and if you ask me I will give you water." Then between herself and her husband – for when she does ask, "Sir, give me this water," he says to her, "go and fetch your husband and come back".

We pray "the grace of our Lord Jesus Christ . . . be with us all"; we ask for that free gift for ourselves but also for others, so that it may pass to and fro between us. What we are asking for is glory ... "the grace of Our Lord Jesus Christ, and the love of God, and the fellowship of the Holy Spirit", the dance of love which is the essence of the Godhead; we ask for the double gift of grace, that the glory may spring out of the secret centre of each one of us, and give us to each other.

6

Death: "By death trampling on death"

Jesus expressed in a number of vivid images the purpose or which his Father had sent him. "To set free prisoners." "To open the eyes of the blind." "To save sinners." They all point to the same reality, but the most challenging image of them all is "to raise the dead". This was not some private purpose of his own but the will of his Father, the very central purpose of the creator for which the universe had been created. "To raise the dead."

He uses the word death in two senses. First to describe the physical death of the body. Secondly, to describe the spiritual death of the person – because that person is dead who does not know God in the to and fro of love. Combining these two senses Jesus says, "Let the dead bury their dead". Not only the corpse in the coffin is dead, but also the minister of religion officiating at the funeral, and the mourners standing round at the burial. The dead are burying the dead. We must explore these two senses of the word death.

First, there is the physical death of the body – our own body, or the bodies of those we love. Confronted by our own physical death, natural human beings experience horror; we shall have to let go of everything to which we cling; we shall have to let go familiar structures and ideas and be swept into the unknown; we shall have to let go our own memory so that we can no longer be conscious of our own identity. Equally, confronted by the death of those we

33

love, we are overwhelmed with horror and grief. We had
become one with them, woven together, giving life to each
other. Now with their death we too have died, and there is
an awful emptiness in which there are not even words left
in which we can mourn them. I remember when my first
wife died discovering that the only line of poetry which
expressed my anguish was King Lear's cry, "Oh! Oh! Oh!
Oh! Oh!"

Secondly there is the spiritual death of the person. I grow
hard inside. I am no longer able to love, so that the very tap
root of my being is cut. I can no longer know God, so that
the spring inside me dries up. This may be the result of
being too busy, or clinging to power and to my own reputation – or it may be brought about by the materialism of the
society in which I live. For one reason and another I have
"missed the mark" for which I was created, which (as we
have already seen) is the definition of sin. I have ceased to
be a person, living in community with other people. "All of
us together", says St Paul, "have sinned and have fallen
short of the glory of God" – we have been seeking our own
glory instead. But "the wages of sin", he warns us, "is
DEATH". For the work I have been doing I have already
been receiving my weekly wage packet, or perhaps a salary
cheque paid more genteelly and discreetly into my bank
account, and those wages, that salary which I have earned,
is DEATH. It is separation from God.

But there is another aspect to death. I learnt it from a
Russian lady, Julia de Beausobre, who as a young woman
had been tortured in a concentration camp and had written a
book about her experience called The Woman who could not
Die. As she approached in old age her own physical death
she said to me, "the moment of death will be the inrush of
timelessness". We all have some knowledge of what she
meant by timelessness. When we are relaxed on holiday and

clocks and watches no longer tyrannise us, and above all
when we are with the person or the people we love most and
are no longer conscious of time, then another and a deeper
quality of life begins to take over. It is eternal, and the word
"eternal" does not mean time going on and on for ever, but
"timeless" – a quality of life not imprisoned in time. So
Julia, as she approached the death of her body, was
conscious of timelessness like a great reservoir of water held
back by a dam, and she felt that now the frail little dam
which was her body was breaking, and timelessness would
come rushing in. Many people who are dying have a similar
experience of some joy or somebody they love coming to
meet them out of the darkness of death. My sister Marjorie
said in the last moments before her death, "this is going to
be exciting", and her son, my godson Martin, who died of
cancer in his early twenties said, "I feel that I am setting out
on the adventure of happiness". As my first wife Scilla was
dying, Cecily Saunders the founder of the hospice
movement told me this – "We accompany them as far as we
can. Then we have to let them go, knowing that they will be
met".

The same appears to be true as we experience that more
terrible death which is the spiritual death of the person. As
we are being paid the wages of sin, in the very heart of our
emptiness and our separation from God, we experience love
coming to meet us. When we can no longer pray, when the
spring of love dries up within us, when we discover the
power of evil in ourselves and in other people dividing us
and tearing us apart, then paradoxically we are in the right
place. In some miraculous way, death reveals to us the secret
of life. *Our separation from God is an essential gateway to
our communion with him.* "Those who sit in darkness and in
the shadow of death" – only those have cried out with the
whole of themselves, and from the deepest depths of their
human need, "Save us! Help us! Deliver us from evil!",
only they know that in the darkness love has come to meet

them – "the dayspring on high has visited us ... to guide our feet into the way of peace".

These twin truths are focused in the death of Jesus. First, that confronted by death he experiences the horror of death. At the tomb of his friend Lazarus he pants and trembles — the Greek word is that used for the snorting and trembling of a horse in the presence of something which terrifies it. So Jesus "panted and trembled in his Spirit", not only in his human psyche, but in that secret centre of himself where he met God; "he confused himself" – his True Self was churned up like a rough sea; "Jesus wept". Again we read that in the garden of Gethsemane "being in agony, he prayed more urgently, and his sweat became like great drops of blood falling to the ground". He is entering the darkness not only of physical death but also of spiritual death. St Paul expresses it in a startling paradox: "Him who knew no sin, God made him to be sin on behalf of us". As the representative of our sin and separation from God he cried out on the cross, "My God, my God, why have you forsaken me?"

But woven into that horror was the twin truth, that out of the darkness his Father was coming to meet him. For finally he said, "Father into your hands I entrust my Spirit". He sees the Father running to meet him, like the Father of the prodigal son in his own parable, with hands held out to welcome him home. Into those hands he entrusts his Spirit – for us.

The Orthodox Church, looking in wonder at this death, bursts out into the great hymn of Easter Day "By death he has trampled on death". In the next chapter we must expose ourselves to the mystery of resurrection, but for the moment remember that there is no resurrection except from death. It is by death that he tramples on death. Through separation from God he has entered into communion with God. By letting go he has set us free. By suffering he has entered into glory and given us to each other.

7

❀

Resurrection: Life through death

Some years ago I was asked to chair a debate at King's College, London, on the question "Do we believe in life after death?" The opening speakers were a biologist who said, "No, it's an impossible contradiction", and a theologian who said, "Yes, it's at the very heart of our faith". Summing up at the end of the debate I suggested that Christians don't believe in life *after* death, they believe in life *through* death. "After" is a time word, and we do not believe that if we die on Tuesday our life as we have experienced it in time and space continues somewhere else on Wednesday. What we do believe is that, through a real death of the physical body, our life can be transformed and raised up by God into a new quality of life called eternal. So we come to the word RESURRECTION.

Resurrection, in New Testament Greek, is *anastasis,* which means literally "standing up" *(stasis:* standing, *ana:* up). The English words "standing up" have a twofold meaning – they can refer to what I do with my own body, "I stand up", but also to what I do with something else, for example "I stand the ladder up against the wall, I raise it up". Similarly the Greek word *anastasis* can mean "standing up" or "raising up". At the resurrection of Jesus, God raised Jesus up "from the dead", which means literally "from the corpses". Jesus was utterly dead. The secret at the heart of his life had been "of myself I can do nothing – but my

Father gives me everything", and now at his death that to and fro of love between him and the Father came to its final perfection. Jesus was nothing, empty, broken, and his Father sprang up out of his emptiness, and flowed through his brokenness, and raised him into heaven to be the Lord of the whole universe.

In Luke's record of events Jesus died on a Friday, lay in a tomb on a Saturday, and was raised on the Sunday; forty days later he ascended into heaven, and on the fiftieth day (Pentecost = fiftieth) he came again, and entered into the lives of his disciples. But John, in his gospel, seems to imply that all these events are one single happening. They are stretched out in time so that our minds can grasp them one by one, but from God's point of view in eternity they are one truth, and each of them a necessary part of that truth, enfolded in the one single whole.

How can we speak of this one truth? Paul writes of it as a "New Creation". Jesus, raised from the dead, has become the focal point of a new creation of the whole universe. If we understand the first creation of the universe in terms of a "big bang", then we might picture the resurrection of Jesus as a second big bang. At the first big bang the whole universe exploded out of nothing, and in a tiny fraction of a split second was flung out on its course in a wonderful order, and in the four dimensions of space and time. Scientists suggest that there may have been ten other potential dimensions which were not in fact realized. As we struggle towards a picture – it can only be an image – of what this second "big bang" could mean, we might say, "another potential dimension has been realized". Now, around Jesus, the whole creation can realize what it has always been potentially – it can become a five-dimensional universe, and the fifth dimension is the Love of God dancing between the creator and his creation. What has happened

38

at the resurrection of Jesus is a marriage of heaven and earth.

"I saw a new heaven and a new earth", writes the author of the Revelation, the last book in our bible. It is not only the physical order in which we live that has been made new, but also the spiritual order in which God lives. Both of these orders, as they enter into the dance of love with each other, are transformed. Their potential is realized. Now there is "joy in heaven . . . joy in the presence of the angels of God", and on earth God's love set free to flow out of the bellies of human beings, and his glory to be revealed through every blade of grass and every slug. "Behold, I make all things new."

The resurrection stories are trying to describe the "New Creation" in the language of the old creation. The very words have to be transformed by the inner reality of this marriage A heaven and earth, and understood in a new and two-fold sense. What "really" happened is no longer what human eyes could see in a four-dimensional universe. The words re describing the *new reality*, in which things on earth and things in heaven are woven together into a new context. Mary Magdalene sees two piles of graveclothes, "the linen clothes lying there, and the handkerchief that had been around his head, not lying with the linen clothes, but folded together in place by itself". Then she looks again, and she sees "two angels in white, sitting one at the head and the other at the feet where the body of Jesus had lain". What did she really see? Then she turned, and "saw Jesus standing there, and did not know that it was Jesus". She supposed him to be the gardener. Similarly, in the afternoon, two disciples were walking to Emmaus, and "Jesus himself drew near and went with them, but their eyes were restrained so that they did not know him". It was not until he took bread, blessed it, broke it and gave it, that their eyes were opened and they knew him. Again by the Lake of Galilee "Jesus showed himself to his disciples". A fisherman invited them to breakfast. Then we read the extraordinary words, "None of the disciples dared ask him 'Who are you?' – knowing that it was the Lord".

What, who, did Mary and those other disciples see? Was it a real gardener, a real traveller, a real fisherman, who reminded them of Jesus? Or was it the real Jesus, looking like a gardener, a traveller, a fisherman? This dichotomy belongs to the old creation. In the new creation we must be bold to say it was the real Jesus in a real gardener, a real traveller, and a real fisherman. This is the big bang that must happen in our own minds and hearts, to match the big bang which happened in Jerusalem, and reverberates through the whole creation. The truth is both objective and subjective. Jesus has both transformed the reality, and opened our eyes to a new way of seeing it.

I came to the edge of this mystery when my first wife died, and though I have told the story before I must tell it again, knowing that many people can tell similar stories from their own experience. She had had an operation for cancer some months before, when her pituitary gland was removed. "I feel I have lost my horse", she said – my energy, my spirit. A week or so after her death my children and I went on holiday to Anglesey and were walking round the cliffs at Rhoscolyn where I have been almost every year of my life. We came over a rise and saw in front of us a horse, two fields away, in a place where I have never seen a horse before or since. It raised its head, whinnied, and came galloping through a gap in the wall and across these two fields to meet us at the stile we were just about to cross. It was a mare, in foal, and she licked our hands. I knew, with that inner clarity which comes through the experience of death, that in and through that real horse my wife, my children's mother, had come to us. She was saying, "Look,

I've got my horse back! I'm so happy you are on holiday, and I am with you". This was both an objective and a subjective experience. From the other side of death somebody had taken an initiative. The real presence of my wife had come to us in the body of a real horse. She had spoken to us through a symbol which to those who loved her was charged with the meaning of her death and resurrection.

The reality of the New Creation into which Jesus calls us is intensely intimate. "Mary!" he says. We are called into an intimate to and fro between the deep centre of our own humanity and the deep abyss of God's love. "Do not cling to me", he says to Mary. "Do not cling to me as you have known me in the past as your teacher. You must let go of everything, even of me the risen Christ. Why must you do that? Because 'I ascend to my Father and your Father'. Round me everything will be made new, and will become alive with a new meaning. I am inviting you to come with me, and to be raised up into that New Creation. Get up and go to my brothers and sisters, and become the messenger (the angel) of the New Creation. As you go, I will be with you."

On Easter morning he spoke to this one woman, and transformed her consciousness of the whole universe and of who she was within it. In the evening he came through locked doors and stood amongst his disciples and transformed them into a community of his brothers and sisters. He set them free and gave them to each other. Then he sent them out as his representatives to transform the world. He breathed his Spirit into them. He defined their purpose, which was to set people free – to let go people's sins, so that they might become their true selves, and finally the whole creation might become the New Creation that it is meant to be.

The resurrection of Jesus, the marriage of heaven and earth, is only completed when what happened in him is reproduced in us. As we do the truth, we shall come to know the truth – the truth of life through death. So we have been told by him who said, "I AM the resurrection".

8

Prayer: Lovers meeting

When he was Archbishop of Canterbury Michael Ramsey once said, "People ask me for a national day of prayer, and I know that what they want is to bombard God. They think that if we bombarded him all together, we might persuade him to change his mind". That brings us to another of the key Christian words which, as the Archbishop shows us, have lost their meaning – PRAYER.

There is a peninsula in northern Greece called Mount Athos, where monks have been praying for thirteen hundred years or more, and rediscovering day by day the heart of true Christian prayer. Instead of bombarding God they enter with Jesus into the mystery of his death and resurrection – the mystery of God's love flowing through his emptiness.

They pray the Jesus prayer, "Lord Jesus Christ, have mercy on me the sinner". They say it not once, nor a hundred times, but continually. Sometimes the words of the prayer become one with their breathing – "Lord Jesus Christ" as they breathe in – "have mercy on me the sinner" as they breathe out. Gradually the prayer passes beyond words and becomes a new consciousness – a new way of knowing one-self, and of experiencing everything else.

One summer night about twenty-five years ago, as we sat under the stars on the roof of his monastery, an Abbot told me about that way of prayer. "I pray it most deeply at night", he said, "when everything is still and empty. As I pray, three things happen. First, it is ME and HIM. Then it is HIM and ME. Then it is only HIM." After twenty-five years I begin to understand what he meant.

First it is ME and HIM. "Have mercy on ME THE SINNER." The sinner, as we have already seen, means the one who has missed the target, and the target is LOVE. I was created to love and be loved, and this is what I long for above anything else in the world, but what I fail to be and do. The words "Have mercy on me the sinner" are a quotation from the parable of Jesus about the Pharisee and the publican who went up into the temple to pray. While the Pharisee congratulated himself on being so good, the publican cried out of his inner agony "have mercy on me the sinner". Note that he says *the* sinner, not *a* sinner. Everybody in that town knew that he was the wickedest person in the place. So it is with each of us as we stand before the love of God.

What is the root of this sin for which I ask mercy? The Jewish-Christian tradition calls it spiritual pride, by which (like Satan) I put ME in the place of God, ME who clings to power or money or reputation, ME who clings to other people and tries to control them, ME who clings to my religion and wants to manipulate God. But Jesus pointed to a deeper root within the heart of that ME, to a pain which I dare not face, and to a fear which makes ME cling on so desperately because I am too frightened to let go – like someone hanging over an abyss or being sucked into a black hole. The pain is that I am rejected, and the fear that I cannot be loved. Spiritual pride like that of the Pharisee can be a defence mechanism against that terrible discovery.

As I begin the Jesus prayer I cry out like the publican "have mercy on ME". I pray urgently as one who is lost. I pray like a prisoner who cannot escape from his prison. I ask, and search, and knock. I can offer to God nothing except my emptiness and my longing. Have mercy! Look on me and understand me! Come to me and be tender towards me! For I can only let go into your merciful arms if they are ready around me.

*

44

Then, in answer to my prayer he comes, and I turn away
from myself towards HIM – the LORD JESUS CHRIST. He
is JESUS – a part of our human history, the one who -cried
out on the cross, "My God! Why have you forsaken me?"
He is all compassion, and has shared our ultimate pain and
fear, and is beside me now in my emptiness.

He is LORD – the centre of the new creation of the whole
universe, round whom everything is seen in a new light. In
that new creation God's glory is shining through everything
that happens, and springing out of the personality of each
human being. Most astonishing of all, it is springing out of
the depths of myself.

He is CHRIST – the word Christ means literally the
anointed one. He is the one sent by God to bring in the new
age of justice and peace on earth. He hears the cry of the
poor, and comes to set things right. He is leading the
nations out beyond security into that dangerous state called
peace, where everyone is set free to be their true selves and
belong to each other.

These three words, LORD JESUS CHRIST, open up an
inexhaustible treasure, and are a fountain of healing from
which we can drink afresh every day; for as when we draw
back the curtain in the morning the light is already in room,
so in the very moment that we pray for mercy he has already
given us mercy, for he is mercy.

Then we begin to understand the dance of love which is
at the heart of prayer, that not only are we searching for
him, but also that he is searching for us. He is like the
father in the story of the Prodigal Son who, when his son
came stumbling home but was still a great way off, saw
him, and had compassion, and ran, and put his arms round
him and kissed him. Now the son can stop clinging to his
guilt for the past and his fear for the future, and he can
let himself go into the arms of love which are already
around him.

*

"Then", the Abbot told me, "it is only HIM". I hesitate before those words and the mystery they signify, remembering that "those who know don't say, and those who say don't know"; but I must try to say what I don't yet know. I think that at this third stage of the prayer the first two stages have come together, my emptiness and God's Love. Now God's Love is flowing out of my emptiness.

Jesus has given us a picture through which we can approach this truth. He says, "I AM the vine, you are the branches. Dwell in me and I in you", for if a branch dwells in a tree and is attached to the stem of the tree then the tree dwells in the branch, and the sap flows through the tree and into the branch to produce the fruit.

Now it is only HIM, who says "I AM the vine"; and now this I AM is dwelling in each of the branches – the to and fro of love between the Father, the Son and the Holy Spirit is dwelling in you, and is dwelling in me. We belong to each other. You are in me and I in you. The whole creation dwells in each one of us, and we are in every part of it. There is no need to bombard God. As we pray "Lord Jesus Christ have mercy on me the sinner", the words become an exclamation of joy. We are asking it for each other, and receiving it for each other; the Jesus prayer has become intercession, and intercession has become one with thanksgiving because the gift we ask for has already been given. God's love flowing through our emptiness gives us to each other, and this communion is beyond time, so that when St Francis prays, "grant me to know the suffering of Christ on the Cross and the Love of Christ on the Cross" he prays it for us, and receives for us what he has asked for.

Ten years later I met the Abbot again, and he led me deeper into the heart of the Jesus prayer. I couldn't have understood it on the first occasion – not until I had been stumbling for years along that way and losing the path and being brought back, and was beginning very reluctantly to recognize that

God's love flowed out of my emptiness. The Abbot told me, "when you pray the Jesus prayer you receive the Lord's Prayer".

This is an amazing truth, which when you come to see it is obvious. If we pray "Jesus have mercy", then because he is mercy he will give us himself. He will give us his spirit which is the to and fro of love between the Father and the Son, and he will give us his prayer which is the meeting of those two lovers. We call his prayer the Lord's Prayer, and in it the Lord of the new creation gives thanks and intercedes for us. The LORD JESUS CHRIST is praying for us, the vine for the branches, but not for us as objects who are outside himself. He is praying in us, on behalf of us all, as our representative.

As we receive that gift of the Lord's Prayer it will begin to flow through our emptiness as it flowed through his emptiness, and to pray itself. Then our prayer will be "to the Father, through the Son, and in the power of the Spirit", which is the traditional definition of Christian prayer. We shall be thanking God for his glory – Father, glorify us that we may glorify you. Let your peace be on earth as it is in heaven – and we shall be interceding for each other – give us bread, earthly bread and heavenly bread, fresh every day. Give us courage to let others go, so that we may be free. As we come to know you in our hearts, rescue us from spiritual pride, and keep us empty so that your glory may spring out of our emptiness.

Then there is only HIM – but no longer even HIM as an object in the accusative case. I AM, he says. I AM is the sap flowing through the branches, so that now there is no longer ME THE SINNER, who was also an object in the accusative case. That ME was dead, but I AM alive. That ME was lost but I AM found. Now there are only two subjects – two lovers meeting.

9

Love: Ecstasy

In the university library at Oxford there is a strong box, or treasure chest, presented by Sir Thomas Bodley who founded the library about 1603. Under the lid of the chest there is a beautifully-wrought assembly of locks and bolts which are all operated by one master key, so that as you turn the master key they all spring open.

In the last eight chapters we have been trying to rediscover the original meaning of some key Christian words, which can open the treasure chest of the mind and heart of Jesus. We began with GLORY, the dance of love within the Godhead, in which we human beings are invited to join. Then, as we looked at seven other key words, we discovered that GLORY is the master key which enables all those other words to spring open and reveal their meaning. *Repentance* is the door into glory. *Forgiveness* sets us free to enter glory. *Sin* is to fall short of glory. *Death* is the way to glory. *Resurrection is* the coming of glory "on earth as it is in heaven". *Prayer is* receiving the glory, and letting the glory overflow.

If glory is the dance of love, then we must come finally to that most crucial of all words – LOVE; but we discover to our dismay that this word, which gives meaning to all the other words of our Christian faith, has itself lost the original and unique meaning given it by Jesus.

"Greater love has no one than this", said Jesus, "that he lay down his life for his friends" – so his words are generally translated into English. But this is not exactly what we read in the original Greek. The Greek word translated "lay down" is *tithenai* which means simply to put, or to place.

49

The Greek word translated "life" is *psyche,* meaning the soul or the self – it is a complex word meaning the centre of our self-conscious life, of all our feeling and thinking, of our memory and desire and will. Jesus is telling us that the greatest love is "to put your psyche on behalf of your friends". "The good shepherd", he says, "puts his psyche on behalf of his sheep"; this could mean that he puts all his energy and skill at the service of his sheep, and it could mean that he lays down his physical life for them if they are attacked by wolves. Essentially Jesus is telling us, out of the depth of his own inner knowledge, that the greatest love is to put your psyche into the hands of God and to receive it back for your friends. The greatest love is to let yourself go into God's love, so that his glory may spring out of your ego-self, and transform your egocentricity not just into the service of your friends but into a to and fro of love with them.

This to and fro of love is the heart of his own experience. "I AM the good shepherd", he says, "and I know my sheep and my sheep know me, just as the Father knows me and I know the Father". It can also become the experience of his friends, as I have seen for myself in the l'Arche homes for the mentally handicapped, where young assistants come expecting to serve the mentally handicapped, and find themselves caught up into deep relationships with them.

God's love is different from our love. The Greek word for our egocentric human love is *eros,* and Socrates defines *eros* as desire which is searching for wholeness and happiness –it seeks to possess the object of its desire, and to be united with it, and to hold onto it for ever. The New Testament writers had to find another word to describe a love which is radically different from *eros* and which they had seen in Jesus. They call it *agape,* using a rather colourless Greek word which was lying ready to hand for them but was little used, so that they could clothe it with a richer and deeper meaning. *Agape* in classical Greek seems to have had the two aspects of receiving and giving – first of respecting people, and accepting them as they are with affection, and secondly of showing this affection by outward and practical signs of love. St Paul in his song to *agape* proclaims this twofold nature of Love. "*Agape* suffers long and is kind" – it is very patient and full of practical kindness. But then he leaps beyond the classical Greek meaning of *agape*. He .uses the word to describe the love of God, which we human beings have to receive from the Spirit of God as a free gift. St John goes further still and says "God is *agape*".

The danger is that when we say "God is Love" we may mean our own erotic love – our egocentric desire. This is a particular hazard in the second half of the twentieth century and in the affluent west. Day by day our advertisers stimulate us to desire more and more objects, holding out the promise that if we satisfy these desires we shall find happiness, and every morning our daily newspapers tell us that love means sexual love, and that a lover is somebody with whom you have sexual intercourse. So "God is Love" comes to mean "God is *eros*", or even that our own egocentric erotic love is God. We suppose that God is an indulgent and all-powerful daddy who will give us endless treats, or a fairy-godmother who will grant us all our wishes if only we say we believe in fairies, and when this happy result fails to materialise we say "I can no longer believe in God".

There is a radical difference between *eros* which is egocentric and *agape* which is to "put one's psyche on behalf of one's friends", and Greek had two words for these two different kinds of love. English has only one, so that we declare in our worship "God so loved the world", while at the same time a boy and girl who are attracted by each other say, "I love you". Similarly in Welsh, the word "cariad" expresses both kinds of love. "Cariad tri yn un" (Love three in one) describes the essence of the Trinity, while "cariad" also means "my darling". Why is it that we British recognize these two kinds of love to be radically different, yet at the same time we stubbornly refuse to distinguish them in our language?

The answer in the Jewish-Christian tradition is that *agape* created *eros* – "God created mankind in his own image, male and female created he them" – and consequently *eros* has within itself a potential, and indeed a natural tendency, to develop into *agape*.

If we look at our own experience of erotic love we find this to be true. When two people fall in love they seek, as Socrates said, to possess the object of their desire and to be united with it and to hold onto it for ever. In the confident illusion that this will happen a bride and a bridegroom may promise on their wedding day "to love and to cherish till death us do part", but from the first day of the honeymoon they will discover that husbands and wives cannot possess each other. Then over the years they may learn, as they clash and quarrel and forgive, to respect each other as unique persons and to set each other free; they may learn, as babies are born, to put their psyches on behalf of their children" in all sorts of practical actions, to support and enjoy them for 20 years and then to let them go; they may learn, as they themselves grow older, to grow together in compassion, in gratitude, and into the ultimate mystery of death. The journey of love on which they were launched by *eros* turns out to be the school of *agape,* in which they are learning to lay down their psyches and to lose their egocentricity in each other. This spiritual truth of *agape*-love is reflected from the very beginning of the journey in the most natural and carnal act of erotic love, for as they have sexual intercourse together they may from time to time, and on occasions which are not altogether under their control, arrive at a climax of ecstasy where their separate ego-selves are lost in the to and fro of love between them.

Eros and agape meet in ecstasy. This word ecstasy (the noun and the verb) occurs twenty-four times in the Greek text of the New Testament, but not once in the English translations. In Greek *ekstasis* means, literally, "standing out". It is the state of being outside one's normal mind. It is translated in English amazement, astonishment, or being beside oneself. The word ecstasy describes the reaction of the onlookers when they are confronted with the miracles of Jesus – when a blind and dumb man speaks and sees, when Jairus' daughter who was dead stands up, when Jesus walks on the sea. The foundations of their minds are shaken, and things are happening which can no longer be understood in old categories. At the resurrection of Jesus the women "fled away from the tomb, for trembling and ecstasy had taken hold of them". On the day of Pentecost Jews from all over the world, as they saw and heard the disciples, were in ecstasy and astonishment. Both Peter and Paul were "in a state of ecstasy" as they received their call to go out to the Gentiles. At all these turning points people are being challenged to "stand outside their normal mind" and to let go their ordinary way of seeing things, to put their psyche into the hands of God, and to be transformed in their feeling and thinking, their memory and desire and will. This, as we have already seen, is a description of repentance.

As human beings approach God they have to enter this state of ecstasy. What is even more astonishing, as God approaches human nature he too chooses to enter into a state of ecstasy. He leaves the security of heaven and of eternity, and makes himself vulnerable in time and space. He enters into a new depth of compassion, no longer just empathising with us from a safe distance but actually sharing our suffering, and into a new height of joy, for as he comes to meet us and we respond to him "there is joy in heaven over one sinner who repents". Our repentance is to enter into that ecstasy with God.

Ecstasy is not of itself the meeting point of *eros* and *agape*. St Paul tells us that ecstatic speech without *agape* is "sounding brass and clanging cymbals" – it is *eros* disguised as religion, and just so much senseless noise. *Agape,* he says, accepts other people and sees the good in them. *Agape* goes on for ever. Beyond that he can only say what *agape* is not. It is not arrogant, not greedy, not irritable. As his list of negatives gets longer we want to cry out, "Stop! I am all these negatives! I cannot love!"

Then, in answer to our cry, Love comes to us, Love who is the climax of ecstasy. The word climax means literally a ladder, though generally today we use it to describe only the top rung of the ladder. That ladder between earth and heaven which Jacob saw in his dream, Jesus declared himself to be. In him *eros* is lifted up to heaven and *agape* comes down to earth, and both have become ecstatic, reaching out beyond themselves. The top rung of the ladder is his death and resurrection, when Jesus "lays down his life for his friends" into the hands of God, and pours out the Spirit of the Father for them in compassion and joy.

The last verses of the bible lead us through the death and resurrection of Jesus into the full mystery of our faith – "Christ has died. Christ is risen. Christ will come again". They are a poem which describes his coming again in a dance of love between flesh and Spirit.

> The Spirit and the bride say, "Come!"
> "Surely I am coming quickly", he says.
> Amen. Come Lord Jesus!

Now, in the eternal present, he has come, and he is standing amongst us. He says, "I have brought for each of you an

invitation to my marriage feast, and it will add greatly to the
joy of my Father if you will be part of the company".

God the Father, God the Son,
God the Holy Spirit,

request the pleasure of your company
at the marriage
of

The Love of God
to
Human Nature.

RSVP

55

II
JOURNEY OUT
JOURNEY IN

1

The Spirit of the Age

Journalists, politicians and clergy often refer loosely to the Spirit of the Age. These words correspond to what the Germans call the *zeitgeist*, the spirit of our time, and invite us to explore what is happening within our culture during these last decades of the twentieth century. Where are we, and where are we going? What are the human concerns, interests, problems and opportunities which preoccupy our generation? How do we see ourselves? How would we begin to answer the question, "Who am I?"?

But the words "Spirit" and "Age" have another resonance. They are two of the key words of the Christian scriptures. There the word Spirit refers not to the *zeitgeist*, to the spirit of our time, but to the eternal Spirit, the spirit of Truth which is seeking to express itself at all times and in all places. The word Age refers not to an age in time, but to that eternal order called "the age to come" which is hidden in the depths of every present moment, and which paradoxically is not coming in the future, but is always coming now, in the present.

As these two senses of the words confront each other they stir one's curiosity. Should there be some dialogue between a zeitgeist and the eternal Spirit of the age to come? Through the preoccupations of our time, and through the fluctuations and changing moods of each generation, does the eternal Spirit reveal the truth about the universe and our place in it? Can we today see any "signs of the times"? A sign points beyond itself, as a road sign in Oxford might point towards London, and a sign of the times would be something happening within our culture which points beyond itself, and reveals the nature of the goal toward which we are travelling.

400 BC PARTY FACTION

I start from an experience I had as a student in Oxford some forty years ago. I was struggling to write an essay on Plato's *Republic,* and suddenly, at 11pm, sitting rather exhausted at my desk, I saw Truth standing naked before me. What I saw was this, that Plato was answering the question of his own time, of his *zeitgeist,* and of his own country Greece, where the whole structure of civilisation was falling apart. His contemporary Thucydides, the historian, has described how the struggle for power between the Athenians and the Spartans had its repercussions in each city state. This struggle for power he calls *stasis,* which we might translate division, or party faction. He writes in words that have echoes into our own time: "By the bloody march of this *stasis* the whole Hellenic world was convulsed, struggles being made everywhere by the popular leaders to bring in the Athenians, and by the Oligarchs to introduce the Spartans ... The sufferings entailed by *stasis* were many and terrible such as have occurred, and always will occur as long as the nature of mankind remains the same. *Stasis* ran its course from city to city, increasing in cunning and violence. Words had to change their ordinary meanings, and take that which was now given them. Recklessness was considered as courage. Prudence was cowardice. Moderation was a cloak for unmanliness, and frantic violence an attribute of manliness ... The fair proposals of an adversary were met with jealous precautions and not with generous confidence. Oaths of reconciliation held good so long as no other weapon was at hand. The cause of all these evils was the lust for power. Human nature, always rebelling against the law, gladly showed itself ungoverned in its passion, and above respect for justice." It was against that background that Plato wrote his *Republic,* as an answer to the urgent questions of his day. He was not playing with abstract ideas. He was struggling to build up a new order of justice, where the rulers should seek the good of those over whom they ruled – where they should turn from the unreal shadows of their passions so that the whole body politic might reflect the reality of the Idea of Good. He is advocating a revolutionary change of mind, and the character through whom he calls people to that change of mind is Socrates, who asks them persistent and searching questions, and breaks through what they pretend to be into the discovery of what they really are, till they have to get rid of him. They condemn him to death for subverting their young people.

Out of the *zeitgeist* of 400 BC, and out of the death of Socrates, comes the *Republic* of Plato. It is a sign of the times, in which the eternal Spirit of Truth points out of the catastrophe of his generation towards a vision of the human race living together in justice and peace, and of human nature reflecting the nature of the transcendent good.

TWENTIETH CENTURY MATERIALISM

Let us return to our own zeitgeist and ask, "What are the characteristics of our time?" "What are our concerns and preoccupations?" "How do we see ourselves, and how would we begin to answer the question, who am I?"

One word pushes itself forward, claiming to be the main candidate to express the spirit of our time. It is the word materialism. We appear to be concerned and preoccupied with having things, as though we believe that this would bring us happiness, and as though the answer to the question "Who am I" is "I am what I have". I may decide to buy that car which is advertised on television, hoping that as I step into the driver's seat I will gather from the car the potency which it represents and realise it within myself. Or I may decide to buy that perfume, or that video, or that house, so that I can say not only "I am what I have" but "I am what other people see me to have". Let me get rich, and let my company take over other companies until it becomes a multinational, and until, one day, I become its president. Then with a dozen or so other presidents we shall be responsible to nobody. We shall sit on each other's boards, and none shall make us afraid – until perhaps one of those bastards tries to take me over.

I was recently in hospital, and in the ward with me was one of the vice-presidents of a multinational. He told me how, for fifteen years, he had been living in Hilton hotels. "When I woke up in the morning," he said, "I hardly knew what country I was in." He had been earning a vast salary, which had brought him not happiness, but stress. Now he longed for quiet and solitude, and to rediscover himself. He had begun to know, with Wordsworth, that:

> The world is too much with us; late and soon,
> Getting and spending, we lay waste our powers:
> Little we see in nature that is ours;
> We have given our hearts away, a sordid boon!

Now he wanted time, when he would not be in a hurry – when he could be still, and look at the world around him, and be in tune again with nature – when with Wordsworth he could say (and he quoted these words):

> To me the meanest flower that blows can give
> Thoughts that do often lie too deep for tears.

That vice-president had discovered that "I am what I have" promises happiness but fails to give it. The more we have the more we cling to, and the more we cling to the more we find ourselves the slaves of the very things which we hoped would bring us freedom – like the rich friend of mine whom I met on a lovely summer afternoon, about 2 o'clock, and he said, "I'm absolutely exhausted. I've been spending the whole morning ringing up my stockbroker." We are bombarded every day, in the press and on television, with advertisements, and with the promise of an affluent world in which our troubles will be left behind us; but that picture turns out to be an illusion, and the expectations are never realised. We find ourselves, instead, in a turbulent world where there is a widening gap between rich and poor. However rich we are, there are always people on the next rung of the ladder who are richer. To climb up onto that next rung I must work harder, even though it means destroying my family life. "I am what I have" casts a spell over me, and draws me into the parallel illusion that "I am what I do", and into the absurdity that while millions of my fellow citizens are unemployed I find myself working longer hours, and more frantically. At the same time I have to protect myself against the anger and the increasing violence of those who are poorer than I am – who also watch television – whose expectations are also aroused every day and then savagely frustrated – who look around them at a shoddy rented room in a dirty street where 50% of their neighbours are unemployed and are struggling, with no hope of glossy luxuries and glamour holidays, merely to feed and clothe their children. As they, too, are told "You are what you have" and "You are what you do", they are driven to the conclusion "I am nothing. I am of no value".

But the most terrible consequences of "I am what I have" is that it destroys the tenderness and the joy of our relations with other people. Instead of enjoying people, I want to have them, and I begin to be afraid of them because I fear they will want to have me – like the man who once told me, "I don't speak to my neighbours in case they should take advantage of me". To have people is to use them as objects – objects which inflate our sense of power, or sexual objects, and this perverts the very centre of our personality. When a man says that he has had a woman he is thinking in terms that destroy both himself and her – though he may in fact be crying out of his own sense of worthlessness, for here is his last hope to give himself value.

"I am what I have" subverts our sexuality, and we can hardly begin to examine the surface of our zeitgeist without recognizing that we are obsessed with sexuality, and that the perversions are horrific. A friend who is working for reconciliation in Northern Ireland told me that in a group of girls he was dealing with one in four had been sexually violated in childhood, by their fathers or another member of their family, and a similar picture comes from the USA and from parts of my own country. In the world at large it is alleged that one million children each year are bought or kidnapped for the "porn trade", some of whom are ritually murdered, and their deaths are filmed and shown on video.

This is the ultimate consequence of materialism. People are treated as objects and I, the observer, cease to be a person. I become an individual, standing alone, in despair. "One is one, and all alone, and ever more shall be so."

A POLARITY OF OPPOSITES

But as we look below the surface of our *zeitgeist*, another picture begins to present itself which is almost the exact opposite of the first. *In the realm of our sexuality*, perhaps the outstanding fact of our time is the new partnership which is emerging between men and women. Husbands are seen pushing the pram, and at home are sharing in the cleaning and the cooking. We are coming to the end of a patriarchal age which has lasted some four thousand years, and to understand that our true humanity involves a balance between the masculine and the feminine, a giving and receiving, a trusting each other and needing each other, and that this is true both outwardly in the relation between men and women and also inwardly in the discovery of a proper harmony and interdependence between the masculine and the feminine within the psyche of each person. Many people are saying that the great search in our time is for the discovery of the feminine. My own conviction is that equally urgent is the discovery of the masculine – a true masculinity which can be the partner of a true femininity.

Again, *in the realm of our materialism,* the same paradox confronts us. Two opposites are held together, and we seem to be passing through a sort of paroxysm of materialism which may betoken the end of an era. A young businessman, who has set up a computer company of which he is the managing director, said to me recently "We are coming to the end of the age of materialism. People can buy a computer and have it in the home but they are beginning to ask 'Do I really want one? Does it really help?'" More profoundly, the whole concept of materialism is being questioned, for it has been based on the assumption that what is real is the order of material objects, existing in space-time and independent of the mind which observes it. The word science has come to mean the study of this material order, of those objects which can be weighed and measured; they can be quantified, and it is because they can be weighed that they are real. This concept of reality is being questioned, not only by millions of young people who are searching for what they call spirituality, and are prepared to travel to the Himalayas or to wherever else they believe it can be found, but also by scientists themselves. For some time scientists have been telling us that matter and energy are two ways of talking about the same thing. Now they are realizing that it is impossible to consider an object apart from the mind which perceives it – there is no such thing as an order of observable material objects existing independently of ourselves. In the last few years an increasing number of scientists are suggesting that a mechanistic view of the universe is no longer tenable. A young scientist I was talking to recently in Cambridge, a research biologist, while standing very firmly by the scientific method in which he had been trained to study the physical world, said "I realise that there is also a spiritual world, and I understand that these two meet in the human mind. I can look at the physical world, and see not only quantity in it, but also a quality of beauty. I can give that beauty to it, and draw beauty out of it, which it does not have apart from me."

As materialism begins to loose its grip over us, so we begin to break free from the illusion of the individual – we begin to sense that there is another answer to the question "Who am I?" We are not individuals standing alone, each with our rights; such a creature could never exist, for if we stand alone we disintegrate. It seems more true to say that we are persons living in community with each other. Each person is unique and of absolute value, but we can only realise that uniqueness as we become responsible for each other. I was helped to understand the importance of this distinction by an essay in a volume edited by Solzhenitsyn in which the writer points out how the concept of the individual plays into the hands of the totalitarian regimes. Individuals can be lined up, and ordered about; but this is far more difficult with "persons living in community", a concept which expresses much more accurately the reality of who we are, and which reflects our rediscovery of the nature of the universe in which we live. It is only during the last twenty-five years that most of us have learnt the word ecology, and have rediscovered the ancient truth that every part of the natural world is dependent on every other part. The physicists are now telling us of a universe which reflects this same interdependence, a universe where fields of forces interact and interplay with each other in a mysterious complexity which the human mind can never fathom. This consciousness of interdependence is gradually corning alive within our own hearts and minds, as for example we actually experience the partnership of male and female in our society, in our homes, and within ourselves – or as Bob Geldof gets the young people of the whole world singing together to raise fifty million pounds for the starving in Africa.

Even this superficial look at our *zeitgeist* shows us a strange polarity of opposites which are manifesting themselves in our own generation. The same polarity appears if we look at the fluctuations of the *zeitgeist* both in the short term and the long term.

THE SWING OF THE PENDULUM

To consider first the short term: if we compare the *zeitgeist* of today with that of twenty-five years ago, we would all agree that there was a different popular mood in the 1960s from that which prevails now. There was a feeling of hope, that old patterns were breaking up, and that we were being set free to come alive in a more authentic way. Pope John XXIII called the Second Vatican Council in 1962, and all over the world Catholics began to worship in their own language. At the same time the Beatles rocketed into prominence, and we were launched into an era of pop music in which many of the songwriters were expressing this new sense of freedom. Here, for example, are some lines from a David Bowie record of 1967:

> Happiness is happening ...
> Love cleans the mind
> And makes it Free!!

From that optimism of twenty-five years ago the pendulum has swung. Somebody who travels widely, and studies deeply, and who senses the popular mood of the world today, described it to me as a quiet despair. Certainly, if you compare the students of today with their predecessors in the

1960s they are far more cautious and conservative. Then they believed that they could overturn the system, and that mankind could learn to make love and not war.

Now they keep their heads down and work hard. What has caused this swing of the pendulum? Some suggest that it is economics. Then there was a population boom in teenagers, who had been born after the war; they had a lot of money in their pockets, it paid to promote their culture, and the prospects looked rosy for them all. Now there is unemployment – there is a choice between becoming very rich or being thrown on the scrap-heap, so it pays to be cautious. Others suggest that we see here a swing of the pendulum between the heart and the head. Then we allowed ourselves to feel compassion, but at the expense of accurate thinking, to which we must now return. Or is the swing between the radical and the conservative in each of us – then we were breaking out of the straitjacket of convention; now we are returning to the traditions of our ancestors?

When we look at the long term fluctuations of the *zeitgeist* we get the same impression of a swinging pendulum – or perhaps a better image would be of a metronome, marking the passage of time: its tip points now to the one, now to the other polarity, but its foot stands in some wholeness or total truth which includes both. Five hundred years ago Copernicus was a boy at school. He was growing up in a world that still believed in the cosmology so beautifully described by Dante – the sun, the stars and the planets were circling around the earth, which in time and space was the centre of the universe. Yet beyond time and space, the true centre of the universe was God, the still point, around which everything turned in a perfect order, attracted by his love. The very word universe means everything turning together as one.

It fell to Copernicus to articulate another picture of the universe, and to say, "the earth revolves round the sun. It is not the centre of the universe in time and space". What

Copernicus did, in effect, was to declare that the centre of the universe is everywhere, and that God dwells in the heart of every human being. So from the organic wholeness of Dante's universe he launched us into the age of the individual – into another *zeitgeist* growing out of another picture of the universe – for to the question "Who am I?" there began to be a different answer. Dante had answered, "I am a part of the universe that revolves around the centre of God's love". After Copernicus, European man began to say "I am the centre of the universe". With that new self-confidence there arose a new science, which has led to technical successes which are astonishing; not only have we flown into space and landed on the moon, but we have learnt to transplant our own hearts, and now, through genetic engineering, we seem to be on the edge of controlling the course of evolution itself. But at this very pinnacle of success we are confronted by catastrophe. Not only are we threatening to destroy all life on the earth, so that there will be no evolution to control, but within each of us, in that heart which we have learnt to transplant, there is a cry "Who am I?" I no longer have any picture of a universe in which I can feel at home. I have no cosmology, no macrocosm of which I can know myself to be the microcosm.

THE ZEITGEIST AND THE ETERNAL SPIRIT

So we return to our theme, The Spirit of the Age, and now we must ask ourselves, whether out of the urgent questions and problems of our own time there are arising any answers, as the *Republic* of Plato arose out of the *stasis* of sixth-century Greece, and whether we can see any signs of the times through which the Spirit of Truth is drawing us towards the eternal reality of the age to come, hidden in the depths of this present moment. What is the eternal Spirit saying to our *zeitgeist*?

Part of the answer is that the eternal Spirit always says
the same thing to every *zeitgeist*. As we look at the
teaching of the great world faiths, we find that they are all
confronting us with the same challenge. They are calling
us to a new way of seeing things, to that change of mind
and heart which in Greek is called *metanoia*, and for which
there is no single equivalent English word, since repentance, as I explained earlier (see page 13) unfortunately
means something quite different. Hinduism describes this
world of our ordinary experience as *Maya*, or illusion, and
calls us from unreality to reality, to discover in ourselves
the Atman, the spirit or true self, and to know that it is
one with Brahman the great Spirit. Buddhism speaks of this
world of our experience as *Samsara*, a ceaseless whirligig
of impermanence, confusion and suffering, but declares
that the very fact of being human gives us an exit door
from *Samsara* – the opportunity to awake out of sleep, and
to receive the gift of a new consciousness. Judaism,
through its law and prophets, calls its people to *Teshuvah*,
a return to the God who is the true centre of their life
together, or more profoundly, a return to the living God
who is turning them back to himself and to responsibility
for each other. Christ sums up his message in one word,
metanoia, a change of mind and heart. His final word to
his followers is that they should go and proclaim to every
nation and culture (we might say, to every *zeitgeist*)
metanoia, a new way of seeing things which will make
possible a new way of doing things, a new consciousness
by which they will enter NOW into the "Age to Come".

This *metanoia* to which the one eternal Spirit has been
calling all our different *zeitgeists*, is in the language of the
great faiths the transformation of I into I AM. It is the way
of losing the ego self and finding the true self, of letting go
the I, and receiving the I AM. This letting go of the I
involves letting go of everything that the I clings to and so is
enslaved by – material things, people, reputation, and also

the inner fears and pains, anger and hatred, to which it clings in the secret core of itself. So the I becomes empty and poor and vulnerable. It is on a journey through suffering and into compassion. The I AM, which is received back as a free gift, is the dialogue between the self and the eternal Spirit – it is the to and fro of love between them, in which the self comes to know the Spirit, and to be known by the Spirit, in the same kind of way as a husband and wife come to know each other through making love. In that to and fro, that dance of love, the self is set free, to come alive in the very deep core and centre of itself, to discover that it is one with all created things, and to share in the Spirit's glory.

What sort of dialogue can the self have with the eternal Spirit? I believe that the secret of the dialogue lies in the word glory, and the pattern of the dialogue in the prayer of Jesus, "Father, glorify your Son, that your Son may glorify you".

The eternal Spirit is the to and fro of love between the Father and the Son, as they give glory to each other, but the eternal Spirit is also the Creator Spirit, whose character is reflected in our human nature, and seen in the love of husbands and wives. The dialogue which happens between that eternal Creator Spirit and ourselves is expressed in an old Latin hymn, *Veni Creator Spiritus*. "Come, Creator Spirit, visit the minds of your people, and fill with your divine light the hearts you have created." The next two verses of the hymn ask the Spirit to interact with our own need: comfort us and bring us to life, kindle in us the fire of love, open our blind eyes, give us joy and peace, guide us and protect us from evil. Then in the last verse we pray that in our human minds and hearts which the Spirit has entered we may know the eternal glory of God, and declare it in the depths of each present moment.

Teach us to know the Father, Son,
And thee, of both, to be but one;
That through the ages all along
This may be our endless song,
Praise to thy eternal merit
Father, Son and Holy Spirit.

Some authorities who speak and write about this dialogue give the impression that it is not a real dialogue, because the unchanging Spirit only repeats himself from age to age. Such a Spirit would be like a rather pompous schoolmaster who says, "I have told you before and I tell you again", and the lesson which this schoolmaster-Spirit appears to repeat is "You must lay aside the flesh, and become detached from your human concerns which are only illusions, and be obedient to me". This would not be a real dialogue in which we and the Spirit respond to each other, and are transformed together "from glory to glory". Again, it would not be a real dialogue, because the Spirit would only give and not receive. The words "God so loved that he gave" comfort us, and assure us that his love is a self-giving love; that is the basic truth, and without it there is no hope, but if that is the whole truth, then I feel myself to be diminished by it.

There is a complementary insight within the Jewish-Christian tradition which perceives that there is indeed a true dialogue, and that the Spirit says, "I not only give to you, I also receive from you. When Abraham argued with me, I changed my mind. Your flesh is precious to me. It is in your flesh that I experience new depths of compassion and new heights of joy, and it is out of your flesh that the fountain of my presence will flow. So offer me what you are, and then in the to and fro of love between us I will glorify you, and you will glorify me".

Now if a real dialogue takes place between the eternal Spirit and the self, can we recognize a similar dialogue between the eternal Spirit and the *zeitgeist*? Some might argue that the fluctuations in our moods are of no real significance to the Spirit in the sight of eternity (*sub specie aeternitatis*), and that Macbeth in his moment of despair understood rightly the human predicament:

> Life's but a walking shadow, a poor player
> That struts and frets his hour upon the stage
> And then is heard no more. It is a tale
> told by an idiot, full of sound and fury,
> Signifying nothing.

But as we look into the heart of our own *zeitgeist*, I believe that we can recognize a real dialogue of love actually taking place. The Spirit says, "I am not the changeless Spirit but the Eternal Spirit, who springs out from the depths of each present moment of human history. I am coming to reveal my glory through what is happening to you. As I came to Plato, so now I am coming to you, but you will only understand what I am saying if you recognise the cry I am answering. Now at this moment of crisis, when you have no vision of a universe in which you can be at home, and when you cry out in despair, "Who am I?", I come to reveal to you that my glory is the to and fro of love. This is not only to be seen in the to and fro between persons, it is the idea which created the universe and which permeates and constantly recreates every part of it. My glory is the dialogue between flesh and spirit and between *zeitgeist* and the eternal truth, and I am having that conversation with you now. As Dante showed you, I am the still point round which the turning universe revolves, and as Copernicus led you to see, that still point is within each one of you. Now your own poets and scientists are helping you to understand that at that still point we meet and respond to each other. "At the still point, there the dance is." The universe is that dance of love. As you see that truth you create it, for the universe is not independent of the one who sees it; you receive the power to share with me in the creation and re-creation of the universe by setting free in it the glory which you see in it. As you experience that truth in your own heart you come to know that the answer to the cry "Who am I?" is not "I am what I have", but "I AM what I AM".

A SIGN OF THE TIME

These things can be described in abstract terms, but I think they only have power to transform us as they reveal themselves to us and touch us through a sign of the times. For me one of the most powerful signs of our time has been a community of people called l'Arche. They have set up small houses all over the world where mentally handicapped people and assistants can make a home together. Young people often join l'Arche out of a sense that they want to help the mentally handicapped, but after a while they find that the mentally handicapped are helping them. Many assistants have told me how they discover in the handicapped people an extraordinary simplicity and compassion, and how in their time of need it is to the handicapped they turn. Paulette, a Canadian girl, told me of a day when she had been going through a difficult time of depression; one of the mentally handicapped people had noticed this and said, "Come with me to the chapel". There she sat down beside her and said "Now I can see that you want to cry". Then after a while she said, "Now I can see that you want to be alone, so I will leave you".

L'Arche is a sign of the time because it stands in contrast to our *zeitgeist*, and is a manifestation of the eternal Spirit pointing us towards the true goal of our humanity. In contrast to our materialism it honours the poor and recognises the power of the powerless – for the mentally handicapped are powerless in that they cannot take many of the important decisions affecting their own lives or exercise control over other people. Yet there flows through their weakness a more fundamental power which dictators do not have, to set us free and to bring us to *metanoia*. In contrast to our individualism, the members of l'Arche are developing a form of covenant which is a commitment to the poor and to each other; they are asking, "Who are we together?" – because only through their commitment to each other can they respond to their calling, and do their work, and live the gospel of the beatitudes, "Blessed are the poor, for theirs is the kingdom of God". In contrast to our secularism, they are turning back to the reality of the Spirit, and acknowledging their need to be fed by the Word of God which lies within the words of the different religious paths, and by the sacraments in which heaven and earth meet in a single mysterious reality. The heart of their commitment to each other is God's commitment to them.

Here is the unvarnished translation of a letter which arrived recently from one of the world's trouble spots, where the latest l'Arche house is being set up (I have changed the names in the letter to safeguard their privacy).

"I am touched to see what God has done, through Lucia, during the last months in X. It is overwhelming to see the number of people there who live in a state of abandonment, rejection, despair ... the number of people who let themselves die or who are left to die.

"The south of the country lived this year a dramatic dryness. Children literally die of starvation. Since months, people have been eating nothing but mangoes – and the mango season is nearly over. The international help starts to get through, but in our countries corruption is still a painful reality. At the same time the guerillas steal their fields from the peasants (with the help and blessing of the landowner army) and they have nobody to call on.

"I understand why today is the hour chosen by God

to call into being a little community as insignificant apparently, and hidden, as l'Arche ... as a sign of his tenderness for the poorest, for those without any more hope. It's beautiful to see the network of friends around Lucia who are really the people that God entrusts to her, and I'm touched to see her hands open ready to give everything, to receive everything.

"God must love Lucia in a very special way, and she radiates that love. But God's call on Lucia is also God's loving response to the handicapped people in X. Once again, God shows us how today he still 'sees the misery of his people, he hears their cry', and he answers when the time comes. And God's time has come for X, and for l'Arche, and I sense how privileged I am to be the witness of this".

Here are two stories out of my own experience which show how the mentally handicapped people can bring us to *metanoia*.

The first I have told earlier, in the discussion of metanoia, but I want to remind you of it again in the context of l'Arche – the story of Doris the mentally handicapped woman who cried out that she had been rejected by her family and thrown into an institution, and of the assistant, who incidentally had been an actress before coming to work in l'Arche, who told me the next morning that the cry had pierced into her heart, and stripped away her pretences. "I realized", she said, "that this was also the deep pain inside myself – that I too was rejected. As I recognised it I knew for the first time in my life that I could be loved." Doris was crying out of that ultimate fear and loneliness in every human heart, which Jesus himself entered on the cross when he cried, "My God! My God! Why have you forsaken me?" The handicapped woman and the assistant were standing together at that point of suffering and compassion where the Spirit can set us free and give us to each other.

The second story more directly concerns myself. Some assistants from a l'Arche house in the USA were describing their community, and showing us slides of the people who lived there. One of them, called Pam, had been severely disturbed, and was full of anger and hatred. For ten years they had lived with her and loved her at great cost, and in the end they had to admit failure. She had to return to an institution. As I heard of the hatred and anger in Pam and saw Pam's face on the screen, and heard the story of the failure of love, I discovered that it had pierced through my defences. I saw the depths of hatred and anger in the core of my own personality, and I knew that though I had resisted love, I could not resist the failure of love.

The first story points to the transforming power of compassion. The second to the mystery that we can only reach that power through powerlessness.

I see l'Arche as a sign of our time, through which the eternal Spirit is calling us out of the materialism of our generation to be with him the creators and re-creators of the universe. But such a consciousness could lead us into an enormous inflation of the ego. We can only respond to this calling through *metanoia* – in so far as we lose the ego-self, and discover "who we are together" in the to and fro between our human nature and the love of God, where I is transformed into I AM.

2

Images of God in Prayer

What image have we of God? As we pray, how do we imagine him, or her, or it?

I ask myself, "for whom or for what do I thirst?", like the Psalmist who wrote

> My soul is athirst for God,
> even for the living God.

I ask my fellow travellers "What is this magnet which draws us towards itself? How do we picture or imagine this reality which we call God, and which answers to the deep reality in ourselves?"

Prayer is a love affair with God which is continually deepening. It is a journey which we are travelling throughout the whole of our lives, and it is mysteriously bound up with our living, so that as we grow and change the image of God to whom we are praying has also to grow and be transformed within us if it is to remain a living truth.

In each of us this love affair or journey is unique, but let me start by telling you about four stages of my own journey in the hope that this may help you to recognize similar events or patterns in your journey.

1 I look back to the first stage, and I remember that when I was a child of about three or four I had the image of God as an old man in the sky with a beard. I also remember my mother kneeling by my bedside, after she had tucked me in at night; I felt comfortable and safe and we were saying together the prayer

Jesus tender shepherd hear me
Bless thy little lamb tonight;
Through the darkness be thou near me,
Keep me safe till morning's light.

I have travelled far since then but I have never got beyond
the truth of that evening prayer, and as I grow in understanding I return to it again and again at a deeper level.

2   Then I remember as a boy of twelve getting up at about
5.30 a.m. one summer morning when we were on holiday
on the coast of Anglesey and going up a hill to see the
sun rise over the sea and over the Snowdon mountains.
There, sitting at the top of the hill, was Dick Howard,
who was then Provost of Coventry in the days before the
Cathedral was bombed. He invited me to sit down with
him, and he began to tell me what he was doing. He
called it prayer, but it was quite unlike what I had
formerly understood by this word. He launched me that
morning on the path of meditation, of taking a verse of
the Bible, listening to it, receiving it into my heart, and
then letting it go with me into the day. This became the
framework of my praying for the next thirty-eight years.
Gradually the central image of that prayer became Jesus
on the Cross saying "Father forgive them for they know
not what they do".

3   Then I remember a day when I was just coming up to
fifty. I was at a clergy conference where the speaker was
Archbishop Anthony Bloom, and he told us the story
which he has since published in a book, about the lady
who said to him "I have been praying all my life but I
have never really met God, what shall I do?" He had
advised her "Go home and tidy your room and sit still for
twenty minutes and whatever you do don't pray". As she
sat still, she began to look, and to listen. The silence

grew profound and at the heart of the silence she became aware of a presence. When I heard that story I suddenly understood something which had been growing in my mind over the years. The truth inside prayer was not that I was trying to attract God's attention but that he was trying to attract my attention. He was saying "Stop all that talking, be quiet and listen". Then I began to see that God was coming to me out of the depths of the present moment. As long as I was full of guilt about the past and anxiety about the future I was keeping God out, but if I could be still and know him in the present moment, then he would come to me out of his creation which was all around me, and out of what was happening now, he would come out of good things that were happening and out of bad things that were happening, and most immediately he would come out of the depths of myself. So the image of God became a presence, or Spirit, or fountain of living water springing out of the depths of our own human nature, and I was launched on the way of contemplative prayer. As I stumbled along that way I fell very quickly into temptation, and it was the temptation into which Jesus was led after his baptism. He had heard the voice saying "Thou art my beloved Son". Then we read, "Immediately, the Spirit drove him out into the desert to be tempted by Satan, and Satan said 'Well if you really are the son of God, then turn these stones into bread and perform great spiritual signs and rule over everybody in the name of God'". So I found that the very same spirit who was leading me into contemplative prayer and the knowledge of God springing out of the depths of myself was driving me into temptation that I should become a spiritual "Somebody", exercising a spiritual force.

4 So I come to the fourth great turning point on my journey which was the death of my first wife. When she died the whole world fell to pieces. But in the heart of the agony I

came upon the truth that I had to let go, and I was confronted by the story of Jesus in the garden on Easter morning when he said to Mary Magdalene, "Do not cling to me". She must not cling, even to the risen Jesus; and why not? – because he was not yet ascended to the Father. If she clung to him she would be clinging to the past. She would be clinging to "my Rabbi", a teacher outside herself who would tell her what to do. But now she must get up and go. As she became his messenger he would be with her and in her; he would be present in each present moment, and he would become the power and the truth of God in her own heart. If she would let go, then she would receive back. So through that experience of the death of somebody that I deeply loved I came to know that I had to let go of God, and that the truth of God was no longer something that I could imagine, but something I had to do and to be.

I have shared with you those four stages of my own journey in the hope that you will say, "Yes, that reminds me of things which I have experienced".

THE PATTERN OF THE JOURNEY

Although each of us has a love affair with God which is unique – how else could it be a real love affair? – and although each of us is on a unique spiritual journey, I believe that the overall pattern of these journeys is the same. This pattern unfolds through the life of Jesus himself – through the child born to Mary, the Good Shepherd caring for his sheep, the crucified Christ, the Risen Lord, the ascended Son seated at the right hand of his Father and the Spirit springing out of our hearts. It is the shape of the journey which unfolds each time we say the Creed; I believe in God the Father the Creator, in Jesus Christ crucified and raised up, in the Spirit who gives us to each other, and opens up between us a new quality of life which is called "eternal".

I can see this pattern in my own journey which I have briefly described. Firstly, as a child, I imagined God as an old man with a beard floating above the sky. Secondly, my image was focused on Jesus. Thirdly, on the fountain of the Spirit. Then there was no image, but only life through death.

THE WHOLE IN EACH PART

There is a curious feature about this journey which does not resemble an ordinary journey in time and space, for example between London and my home in Oxfordshire. On that journey I leave London behind, drive through Pangbourne, and after an hour's travelling arrive in Blewbury; but on the spiritual journey when I pass through any stage of the journey I do not leave it behind. It remains present. For example, as a child I learnt to pray to God the Father, whose arms were around me protecting me. Although I no longer imagine him as an old man with a beard sitting on a cloud, the truth remains with me that he is my Father, and I can hope for no more wonderful end to my journey than to rediscover what I knew as a child, that his arms are around me, and that he is welcoming me home. As a child I learnt to pray, "Jesus tender shepherd hear me ... through the darkness be thou near me," and I can ask for no greater comfort as I go through the valley of the shadow of death than to know that he is with me. When I was a child my mother knelt and prayed beside me, I saw God's love in her and she saw God's son in me, and there could be no more perfect consummation of the journey than to enter into the fullness of that communion of love.

So at every stage of the journey the whole truth is

present; as we travel through time eternity breaks into each moment; as we grow we leave nothing behind but it is gathered into a deeper knowledge. The whole truth of Christian prayer, as it has been formulated intellectually by theologians, was present there for me as a child around my bed – prayer to the Father, through the Son, and in the power of the Spirit. That fullness expressed itself again in the second stage of the journey which I have described; now the focus of the image was Jesus, and through the Son human nature was being lifted up to the Father, and the Spirit offered in whom we might realize our freedom. Then again, in the third stage, the picture of God became less clear until the whole business of prayer was turned upside down and inside out; now it was not so much I who was searching for God as God who was searching for me and finding me; there was not so much an image of God as a sense of being thirsty, and then of some presence, some energy, some love springing out of everything and everybody, including myself. The focus was now the Spirit, but still it was the same truth to which I was being led back – the energy of the Spirit was given through Jesus, and was enabling us "to worship the Father in spirit and in truth". Finally, in the fourth stage, our human minds can have no image of God, because we have to let go the ego-self which creates the images and does the imagining. Now the image of God is something we have to be, and which we can only know as we do it. But still we are in the presence of the same truth; the glory of the Father through the Son and in the power of the Holy Spirit is shining around us and through us.

LETTING GO THE IMAGE

This truth that we are each travelling on a unique journey but all of us on the same journey was confirmed to me by the people of Derbyshire, the diocese in which I was then serving as a bishop. I wrote and asked people "When you pray what images of God do you have?" and I got seventy six answers to my enquiry. They were wonderful letters, each different, and each with the ring of truth. I quote from the youngest and the oldest. A girl of twelve wrote "My image of God is a tall, old, grey haired, bearded man who always has his arms reaching out to help us", and a woman of eighty-seven wrote "I have no image of God, he is the loving, caring presence of all the good surrounding us". Many of the letters used this word "presence" and many of them spoke of radiance. Together they confirmed my own experience that during the course of our human lives the image of God changes and finally breaks. This happens not just once but again and again, for no image can be the whole truth. It can only be a heresy, which means literally a part of the truth, and so you have to let it go. If you cling on to it then it becomes a blasphemy, because you are trying to cling on to God with your little human mind. But if you let the image go in a painful surrender which feels like death, then you receive back the deeper presence of God himself, springing out of your heart for the sake of other people.

BREAKING THE IMAGE

It is not so much that we decide to let the image go, but that the image breaks. This truth of the breaking of the image was confirmed to me by my friend, Norman Todd, a priest in the neighbouring diocese with whom I had been at college long ago. He asked me to lead a school of prayer. I hesitated, because I really didn't know how to teach prayer. Then I asked him, "Will you come and lead it with me?" So we agreed to do it together. We started by sitting down for an hour and sharing with each other very simply and directly what we had discovered about prayer over the course of our lives. Each of us spoke for half an hour telling his story, while the other one listened very carefully; we found that this listening helped the one who was telling the story to articulate what he had to say, and it also helped the listener because he heard things true to his own experience which he hadn't before recognized. Now as we listened to each other we found at the centre of each story was something which we called, for want of a better word, the switch. It was a radical change, both of the way in which we understood the word "prayer" and also of the image of God to whom we prayed. For me it had been the discovery to which I have already alluded, that the ground of prayer was not me searching for God, but God searching for me; and for Norman it had been the discovery that prayer was not something he did alone by himself, but that when he prayed he was part of a great company of the communion of saints who were praying in heaven and on earth. So at the heart of prayer we recognized this truth of a switch – or could we call it a turning point? – and at that turning point the discovery not only that our picture of the word "prayer" was transformed but that the image of God Himself had to break –we had to let it go in order that we might receive back something more wonderful and more complete.

We find this picture of the way of prayer is confirmed by the great spiritual writers. Perhaps the most powerful description of the journey of prayer was written by the poet Dante during the years between 1307 and 1321. In his Divine Comedy he travels through hell and purgatory and into paradise. He goes down into the dark regions of despair and confronts Satan himself in the frozen depths of hell. He climbs up the steep mountain of purgatory, and at the entrance of paradise he is met by Beatrice, the girl whom he had seen and loved in the streets of Florence. She guides him into the joy of paradise, and they ascend beyond time and space into the Empyrean, where all the saints and the servants of God out of every generation are seated together in concentric circles in the pattern of a rose. There, in eternity, the whole company of heaven unites in prayer for Dante that he may be able to look into the face of God. So in the power of that prayer he looks, and sees a glory beyond words, the glory of the Father and of the Son and of the Holy Spirit, the glory of the Trinity in unity. He struggles to understand, but his mind can carry him no further. Then he receives as a gift what he cannot grasp – light flashes through his understanding – what he has desired comes to him. His imagination loses the power to imagine, but at that moment he finds himself to be part of a universe which is attracted by God, and revolving around the still centre of God's love:

> my will and my desire were turned by love,
> the love that moves the sun and the other stars.

Dante's great poem brings us, at the end of his journey, to that turning-point which Norman Todd and I were rediscovering in our more prosaic way six hundred and sixty years later, when it is impossible any longer to have an image of God. The mind cannot grasp the truth of what it sees, and even the imagination loses the power to imagine. Then, as the image breaks, and we no longer try to understand, even the meaning of the word turning-point is transformed; it is no longer the point where we turn to God, but it is the still centre of God's love turning us, so that with the whole company of heaven we have become part of the truth towards which we have been travelling.

REJECTING THE IMAGE

In the great religious traditions of the world we find this same truth of the breaking of the image. The foundation stone of Jewish religious practice is the Ten Commandments, which begin with these words, "I am the Lord your God, you shall have no other Gods but me. You shall not make to yourself any graven image or the likeness of anything that is in heaven above or in the earth beneath or in the waters under the earth; you shall not bow down to them nor worship them. For I, the Lord your God, am a jealous God and I visit the sins of the fathers upon the children unto the third and fourth generation". On a very practical, earthy level this Commandment is telling us, "Do not make idols of stone or wood and invest them with supernatural power and worship them". Why not? Because if you do you will be fouling up the very spring of faith. You will be trying to control God. You will be trying to contain Him and to manipulate Him so that you can harness His power to your own little ego, and do what you want to do with the sanction of His authority. Knowing this danger the Jews smashed up any idols or images of God which they found among the peoples round about them; but the danger of making images of God goes much deeper than idols of wood and stone and enters into the secret places of prayer. When we imagine God as an old man with a beard we are trying to contain Him and grasp hold of Him, so that as a child tries to wheedle his parents into giving him sweets or into allowing him to stay up a little longer to watch television instead of going to bed, so we may persuade God to change His mind and to give us what we ask. When the Jews said "You shall make no images of God" they were pointing towards this great truth, that you cannot grasp hold of God either with your intellect or even with your imagination.

The Moslems teach and live the same truth. A mosque is totally bare of images. God is to be worshipped in loving obedience; at certain fixed hours of the day you are to spread out your prayer mat and this will become the sacred ground where you will meet Allah – he is here and he is now. Bow down before him, prostrate yourself before the Lord your God and pray to him, "Thee alone do we worship. To thee alone do we come for help". Moslems who occupied southern Spain for many centuries built a great mosque in Cordova, part of which still remains in its original simplicity. The Christians liberated the city in 1492, and within the mosque built a cathedral which they filled with statues and paintings. When I visited Cordova it was in the mosque rather than in the fussy cathedral that I felt drawn into the presence of God and confronted by the mystery of God.

Many Christians have felt this same revulsion against graven images. In our own history we remember Oliver Cromwell and his puritan armies who went around the country smashing up the images which they found in our churches; they were protesting against the outward worship of idols, against superstition, against the folly of trying to contain the living God in churches made with human hands; but I wonder whether, at the same time, they recognized the need to smash up the idol of God within their own hearts, and to root out that spiritual pride which was the shadow side of their own puritanism.

THE CLOUD OF UNKNOWING

The same truth about the rejection of images comes to us in what I think to be the most beautiful of our English spiritual writings, "The Cloud of Unknowing". It was probably written towards the end of the fourteenth century when Chaucer was writing his Canterbury Tales. The author is encouraging a young man on the way of contemplative prayer, and he says "When you start you will find only darkness and, as it were, a cloud of unknowing". Between you and God there is this cloud, so that you cannot grasp Him with your mind. You cannot think of Him; for God, he says, "may well be loved but not thought; by love He can be caught and held, but by thinking never".

Those who approach God in this cloud of unknowing have to let go of everything else; between them and the whole creation they have to put the cloud of forgetting, and then they must seek for God with their whole heart and mind and strength. They cannot find him through thinking about him, so the author advises them to choose a little word like "love" or "God", and with this word, he says, "you will suppress all thoughts under the cloud of forgetting". Then choose another little word to express what it is in yourself that you want to put away, and he suggests the word "sin". "Cry out this little word", he says, "as a man might cry 'fire!' or 'help!', and might throw into that tiny word the whole of himself, so that anyone hearing his cry would come to his rescue." So, says the author, you must cry ceaselessly in your spirit the one thing, "sin", "sin", "help!", "help!".

Then, he says, use together those two words you have chosen. "Sin, God", or "Sin, Love", "with the knowledge that if you had God you would not have sin, and if you had not sin you would have God". Like Dante he is telling us that we have to arrive at a point where we no longer have an image of God, we can no longer think of Him or imagine Him. Our prayer becomes our desire reaching out to God and seeking only for His love. It becomes our offering of ourselves to God to co-operate with His purpose. But he also warns us to be careful. "Do not overstrain", he says, and do not by some sham spirituality induce within yourself a warm glow which you falsely believe to be God's love. So be humble. "Work with eager enjoyment rather than with brute force." Do not snatch at God like a hungry dog snatching at a bone, but rather play a game with him, like a child who hides from his earthly father, till that father finds him, and takes him in his arms, and hugs and kisses him.

ICONS

But there is another tradition of Christian prayer which appears, at first sight, to take the opposite view. If you walk into an Orthodox Church you will find yourself surrounded by icons. Icon is a Greek word which means likeness, or image, or mirror image. The walls of the church are covered with paintings; at floor level there may be the icons of the saints, and above them icons of angels, and above them icons of the life of Christ – his birth, his baptism in the River Jordan, his transformation of water into wine at Cana in Galilee, and so on through his passion and into his resurrection. Then high up in the dome you may see the icons of the Seraphim and the Cherubim and the twelve apostles seated in glory; and there in the very centre, looking down at you, is the icon of Christ – the Pantocrator, the ruler of all things. I remember the first time that I went to pray the Eucharist in a Greek monastery, very early in the morning. We began by candlelight, and we could not yet see this great company around us; but as the dawn broke we began to see the saints and the angels and with them the whole company of heaven, and we lifted up our hearts with angels and archangels and all the saints and we cried "Holy, Holy, Holy is the Lord"; then, as the sun rose, and the bread was broken, there above us was Christ our Lord holding all things together by his power and coming to us in his mercy.

As our Greek brothers and sisters enter their church they go forward and kiss the icons. To our western eyes it may look like the worship of idols, but in their hearts is a totally different understanding. The icon is not the image of a saint or of Christ which has supernatural power in itself, it is a window into heaven, through which we can look and see the reality of the saints, or of Christ himself, and through which his mercy and his truth can come to us. An icon is not a portrait. If you look at an icon of the Virgin Mary you will see that certain physical features are exaggerated. Her nose

91

and her fingers, for example, appear to be too long. You are not looking at the portrait of a human girl, as you would be in a painting by Raphael, you are looking at the reality of the Blessed Virgin Mary as she is now in heaven. Through the icon you can approach her as she is now in eternity, and she can approach you. There was a period in the history of the Orthodox Church when people were smashing up icons; they were called iconoclasts, and they were protesting against the danger of heretical idol-worship; but the Orthodox Church decided that these iconoclasts were themselves the heretics, and that for the true worship of God we need icons – not idols which we cling on to in place of God, but doors through which God may come searching for us, and we may go in and find his presence. "Christ", says St Paul, "is the icon of the unseen God" (Col 1:15). He is the door through which we come to God and God comes to us. He, the Son of Man, is the ladder upon which the angels are lifting human nature to God and bringing the spirit of God to dwell in our human nature.

JESUS CHRIST THE ICON OF THE FATHER

So to him who is greater than Dante and greater than the author of The Cloud of Unknowing we now turn, and we ask him for guidance on the way of prayer – "Lord teach us to pray". He replies, "When you pray say 'Father'." Jesus gives us the image of God which was the centre of his own prayer. When He prayed he said, "Abba Father", and he gave us authority to use the same image and to pray with him "Our Father". We cannot pray these words rightly in our own power, but only with him; the early Christians recognized this, and understood that it was the great privilege of the newly baptised Christian that he or she might now say "Our Father". As we seek to understand the image of God in Christian prayer, we look with reverence and curiosity into the mind of Christ. He uses, and tells us to use, the word "Abba", which is the first sound that a little child makes as he or she begins to talk, and which we fathers then proudly take to ourselves and say "Look! my child is speaking to me". In English the equivalent word is Dada, in French it is Papa, and in Greek it is Baba; the same word is used in Africa and India; in the Aramaic which Jesus spoke it was "Abba". This word is used all over the world by little children in the security of their own homes as they run to their father and jump onto his knee and prattle away about all their concerns. So Jesus tells us to pray with complete freedom to our "Abba Father", and He continues to use that word until the very last minutes of his life – "Abba", that tender word, in which all the masculine and feminine qualities of parenthood seem to be combined.

But as he grew from a child and through teenage and into manhood the meaning of that word "Father" grew with him. We can see this new dimension in the story of the Prodigal Son, in that profoundly moving verse "While he was still a great way off his father saw him and had compassion and ran and put his arms round him and kissed him". Now it is no longer the little child running to tell the father about his concerns but the father running to welcome his adult son home.

In St John's gospel the image of the Father develops again. As Jesus leaves behind his home and the carpenter's shop at Nazareth and enters on his public ministry of teaching and healing, the centre of his consciousness becomes "I and the Father who sent me". The Father has sent him out as his envoy plenipotentiary, and has given him the Spirit, springing out of his belly with the authority to do the unique and essential work which only God himself can do. Between Father and Son there is a relation of interdependence. "The Son can do nothing of himself, but only what he sees the Father doing", while "the Father loves the Son and reveals to him everything which he himself does".

93

Within that exchange of love and trust Jesus can say, "I and the Father are one".

As Jesus "grew in wisdom and stature and in favour with God and man", did the image of the Father grow in his heart, and was he too on a journey of prayer? Did he begin with the image of an old man in the sky, and then gradually come to know that the Father was searching for him and running out to meet him; and then that the Father was dwelling in his heart and springing out of him as a river of living water? Our own experience of the journey of prayer has been described in the famous lines of T. S. Eliot:

> With the drawing of this Love
> and the voice of this Calling
> We shall not cease from exploration
> And the end of all our exploring
> Will be to arrive where we started
> And know the place for the first time.

Can we believe that there is a similar pattern in the way that Jesus himself travelled; that in him, as in us, the image of God was being continually transformed while remaining always the same, as he returned again and again at a deeper level of understanding to the truth of "Abba Father"?

Indeed we must believe that Jesus shared this experience of letting go the image in order that he might receive it back again, because he himself tells us that this is the inner rhythm of his response to his Father's command. "I have authority to lay down my psyche and I have authority to receive it back again; this command I received from my Father." The psyche is his human consciousness including his image of God, and he lets it go in obedience to the Father so that he may receive back the mature consciousness of "I and the Father who sent me". Finally on the cross he lays down even that consciousness, as he cries "My God, my God, why have you forsaken me?", and he receives back the glory of the Father flowing out of his wounded heart for us.

This letting go and receiving back is the way we have to travel with him to the Father's house. "You know the way", he says, and when Thomas protests "We do not know where you are going, so how can we know the way?" Jesus replies "I AM the way". Then Philip asks of Jesus the very same question with which we began this chapter "What image have you of God, towards which you are travelling, and towards which we can follow you? Show us the Father". Jesus replies, "The image of God is not something I have, or something I think, or something I imagine – it is something I AM".

So we return to our question, "As we pray, what image have we of God?", and now there is an answer, "We have Jesus. Jesus is the icon of God". He is the likeness of God, and the God to whom we pray is like Jesus. But more than that, Jesus is the mirror image of the Father, so that he and the Father mirror each other in their giving and receiving. As Jesus lifts our human nature to the Father, the Father is welcoming our human nature which is coming home. As Jesus receives the Holy Spirit to spring out of his heart as a free gift for us, the Father is seeking to give his Holy Spirit to those who ask him. Looking at Jesus we see in a mirror the Father to whom we pray – the Father who is welcoming us home, and who is seeking to spring out of our hearts.

ICONS OF CHRIST

But we cannot "have the image of Jesus", in the sense that we cannot grasp it or hold it in our minds intellectually. It is a truth that we have to do and be – the truth of the Word made flesh which we have to receive in our flesh. Wonderfully, by the free gift of God, we have a secret room ready and waiting in the depths of each one of us where the marriage of heaven and earth, of Spirit and flesh, can take place. Jesus speaks of it as a room in his Father's house, which he is going to prepare for us, and where he will come and meet us. We will say more about this room later, but now we need only be astonished and grateful that in this secret centre of ourselves, when we have let go of everything else, he comes to us in our emptiness, and sets free in us his truth of "I and the Father who sent me". Being sent, we are set free – not to have the icon of Christ but to be icons of Christ.

THE LORD'S PRAYER

Then out of this secret room at the centre of ourselves there can spring the Lord's Prayer. I have known this truth intellectually for many years, but one night not so long ago, when I could not sleep because of an anxiety and a sense of evil pressing upon me, when I was confused in the depths of myself and was lost and cut off from the awareness of God, then gently and insistently the Lord's Prayer sprang out of the depths of my soul. It brought an amazing happiness, because as it flowed through me the heart and mind of Jesus were flowing through me for other people, and setting me free of my egocentricity. I embraced the prayer as a drowning man might embrace a lifebelt. "Our Father!" It was praying itself around me through the whole creation, prayer to the Father, through the Son, and in the power of the Spirit. In that prayer the potential of the universe was being realized – the reality of the new creation. As I received the free gift of that prayer I became a tiny part of that reality, within the longing of the love of God which was unfolding and singing around me, and within the will of the Trinity that as Jesus was the icon of the Father, so we might become together the icon of Jesus. "We are being transformed", wrote St Paul, "into the same icon of Christ from glory to glory" (2 Cor 3:18).

Images of God in Prayer

The Lord's Prayer flows through us for each other. During the dry weather I have to water my vegetables with a hose – the water flows out of the hose to my carrots and onions and lettuces and peas and beans and spinach, bringing them life. The prayer which Jesus has given us is like that. We can point our true self in the direction we care about, and the Lord's Prayer passes through. "Our Father", his glory, raising our human nature from the dead, his mercy giving us daily bread, forgiving hearts, rescuing us from evil.

To sum up: if we are asked what image of God do Christians have as they pray, we reply "Christ"; Christ is the image of God the Holy Trinity, but we do not have the image, we dwell in the image, and the image dwells in us and comes alive in our love for each other. As we give ourselves to each other and receive ourselves from each other, as we give God to each other and receive God from each other, Christ prays his prayer through us and God sings through us the song of his glory. But again the image breaks. Did I say that the Lord's Prayer was like water flowing out of my garden hose? Yes, but this prayer is not something we can turn on at will like a tap; it is always a free gift. From time to time we pass through periods of drought when we are not allowed to use our hoses, and then we can only look back over millions of years and see that God has not failed to keep alive the green things that are upon the earth. So lie down in peace and take your rest, and one night what you desire will come to you; as you lie between sleeping and waking you will know that the drought is ended, and you will hear the swish and the splash of the rain as it falls again upon the parched earth.

III
THE DANCE OF LOVE

1

❖

Seeing the Wood for the Trees

There is an old saying "you can't see the wood for the trees". When you are walking through a wood, pushing your way through the undergrowth or through a tangle of branches, you can easily get lost if you don't know the shape of the wood, where you got into it, and how you can get out of it.

So I often feel about the Christian Faith; we are surrounded by trees, by those key Christian words we have been discussing, by articles of the Creed such as "he ascended into heaven", and by verses from scripture such as the parable of the Good Samaritan. These are beautiful trees, and as we look at them we are lost in wonder; but we can get lost in another sense, in the multiplicity of the trees themselves so that we become confused about the shape of the wood in which they are growing.

For most of my life I have been studying the gospel of St John, looking at the stories he tells and listening to the conversations which he records. These are the trees, and I can truthfully say that almost every verse in his gospel has answered to some event in my own life, opening up the vision of God and leading into deeper insights about human nature. But what is the shape of the wood? Through all those stories and conversations what is St John telling us? I ask myself, as I approach my 70th birthday, what is the whole truth which has been revealing itself through all those parts; and as I recognize that "the days of a man are three score years and ten", what baton if any have I to hand on to the next runner in the relay race so that he or she may carry it into the 21st century? In the last 8 chapters of his gospel St John writes the story of the death and resurrection of Jesus, and it is here that we find the focus of the good news he has to tell. I want now to look at the outline of those chapters, not to go into detail, for I have done that already in my book "Water into Wine", but to allow the shape of the story to reveal itself and to speak its message. Here, for me, is the secret centre of the Christian faith. Others find it in the first 8 chapters of St Paul's Epistle to the Romans, or in St Matthew's account of the Sermon on the Mount, or in the parable of the prodigal son as recorded by St Luke. All these passages are pointing towards the same mystery, but in our generation and in the crisis through which the human race is now passing I have found that more and more people are rediscovering the original truth of Jesus through the words of John, "the disciple whom Jesus loved".

What are they rediscovering? It is not easy to say, because it cannot be caught in a formula or confined in a definition. A former secretary of mine with whom I had worked many years ago said to me recently, "In those days I was searching. Now I have found what I was searching for, and I don't know what it is". She had never studied theology, but she was expressing the truth at the heart of theology. The truth of God is something you cannot grasp hold of; you have to do it if you want to know what it is, and it has to be given afresh every morning like daily bread. It can only be described in stories and metaphors. When St John wrote about this truth he was telling the story of something which had happened over a period of three days and in which he had been more intimately involved than any other single human being, as on that Thursday at supper he leaned his head upon the bosom of Jesus, and on that Friday he stood by his cross, and on that Sunday he ran to the tomb in the early morning and found it empty. He is telling the story of events which happened in the objective world, such as the arrest and trial and crucifixion of Jesus, but he is using metaphors to convey the meaning of that story, such as "I AM the vine, you are the branches". These metaphors are pictures which help him to interpret the outward events. The truth of the conscious experience which he is trying to convey to us lies in the interplay between the events and the metaphors.

I shall use a metaphor to describe the conscious experience which these chapters of St John's gospel awaken in me – the metaphor which is the title of this book, the dance of love.

When I use the word dance I think of the tradition of ballroom dancing in which I grew up, and of the male and female partners interacting within a rhythm which remains always the same but in a continuous variety of movements. But more vividly I remember Greek folk-dancing in Cretan villages during the war of liberation, the young men of the resistance taking it in turns to lead the dance, leaping and gesturing and showing off their perfect physique and prowess, and then making way for the next young hero; or after the war, an evening in the island of Santorini, when the company assembled in the local taverna, and sat for an hour as the stars came out, drinking wine and listening to the rhythm of the band – then, gradually, one by one, men and women, they got up and began to dance, and in the dance they expressed the mysterious depth and truth of that moment, the firm earth under their feet, the starry skies above their heads, the island and the sea, the vineyards and the olive groves, the traditions of their ancestors alive in them as they moved together in the age-old rhythms, one with nature, and with history, and with each other, and in that communion each person coming alive in the unique shape of their own body, and with their own energy and vigour. It is sad that England has no such living tradition of folk dance. When I attended an international festival of folk-dancing I found every country represented there except the English; there was African dancing and Indian dancing and

American dancing; there was Swiss dancing and German dancing and Spanish dancing, there was Scottish dancing and Welsh dancing – but no English dancing. If the dance of love is indeed an image of the Godhead, then have we English with our inhibitions and our stiff upper lips cut ourselves off from this most natural expression of supernatural love, and from this very earthly experience of heaven?

In chapters thirteen to twenty of St John's gospel we see the dance of love unfolding through many movements, but always with the same rhythm. As we trace the eight major movements of the dance, this inner rhythm reveals itself. It is the marriage of heaven and earth – God's spirit flowing through our human emptiness.

The Eight Movements of the Dance

THE FIRST MOVEMENT: THE DANCE OF LOVE BETWEEN THE FATHER AND JESUS JOHN 13[1-5]

We read that at the feast of Passover, the great festival of liberation, *Jesus knew that his hour had come to cross over from this world to the Father.*

Abba Father! My beloved Son! This had been his self-consciousness since the day of his baptism, when the heavens opened, and heaven and earth were united in the to and fro of love. The Spirit, who is that to and fro of love, had rested upon him and found its dwelling place in him. Since that day he had known himself to be the ladder between heaven and earth on which the Spirit was lifting human nature to the Father, and bringing the grace and the truth of the Father into human nature.

Now "the hour had come"; no longer would he lift up his friends to the Father in longing and hope, he would actually cross over himself from this world into the Father's house bringing his friends with him and arrive at the end and goal of his journey. *Having loved his own who were in the world he loved them into the end* – the Greek word is *telos*, the end, or consummation, or final cause for which they were created.

To do this he had now to lift up to the Father the whole of human nature, the darkness as well as the light. He had to go down deeper than ever before into that darkness, and put into the Father's hands not only personal sin but also corporate evil, not only the failure of everyman and everywoman to live the glory, but also the power politics which in his day crucified people, and in our day locks them up in concentration camps and finds a sadistic pleasure in torturing their helpless bodies. In that moment, sitting round the supper table with his friends, Jesus was conscious of the depths of evil and the heights of love. He knew that *Satan had put it into the heart of Judas Iscariot to hand him over* to the secular power, but that in the same moment *the Father had given everything into his hands*.

Now there is to be revealed to us the theme on which all the other movements will be variations. The Father "had given everything into his hands" – he had given to Jesus the power to recreate the whole universe in a new order, and in that moment Jesus *knew that he had come out from God and was on his way to God*; the authority which had been given him flowed out of the inner being of God, and it was the authority not only to open the eyes of men and women to their destiny, but actually to raise them out of the death of their ego-centricity into that eternal life which is to know God in the to and fro of love. In the consciousness of that authority he emptied himself of what the world thinks of as power. He took off his teacher's robes, and like a slave tied a towel round his loins. Then he poured water into a wash basin, and began to wash the disciples' feet and to massage them with the towel. Here is the mystery of the glory of God revealing itself in the emptiness of Jesus. It is the mystery of love. "Greater love has no one than this, that he should put his psyche on behalf of his friends" – that he should abandon his ego-self for them. Jesus is putting his psyche into the hands of God on behalf of his friends, and pouring out for them his Spirit, which is the dance of love.

We must note that the Spirit or energy which he receives from the Father and pours out for them is not adequately defined as self-giving love. People who are always giving can be as ego-centric as people who are always grasping, and possibly more dangerous, for now their ego-centricity may be disguised in spiritual clothing; they can become like the false prophets against whom Jesus warns us to be on our guard, "They come to you", he says, "in sheep's clothing, but inwardly they are grasping wolves". Jesus is not substituting one kind of ego-centricity for another. His hour has come, and in the agony and the ecstasy of that moment he is surrendering the ego itself into his Father's hands, emptying himself, letting go his role as a religious teacher in an earthly act of practical love, pouring out his soul for others like water into a wash basin.

By doing this he is reflecting the Father. "I can do nothing", he said, "except what I see the Father doing". If he lays aside his teaching robes and washes the feet of the learners – which is what the word disciples means – it is because he sees the Father doing it. God the Father Almighty, the maker of heaven and earth, is like that; he too lays aside his dignity and status as a teacher. He does not try to force his objective truth into our thick heads, but he gives himself to us in acts of humble service; he laughs with us and weeps with us, and he invites us to know him in our hearts through an interaction and an interplay between us. It is this knowledge that Jesus has received from the Father, and in the to and fro of this relationship he and the Father are one. They need each other. That is the pattern of how things potentially are in the universe, and of how God means them to be.

THE SECOND MOVEMENT: THE DANCE OF LOVE
BETWEEN JESUS AND HIS FRIENDS JOHN 13 [6-35]

The relation between the Father and Jesus will now be reflected in the relation between Jesus and his friends. They will come to know that "he has put everything into their hands", and that they have been sent out by him to share in the creation of a new universe. But they will only be able to know this in their emptiness.

As Jesus kneels before them like a servant, he meets first with embarrassment and rejection. *"Do you wash my feet?"* says Peter. "You are the Lord and Master, and I am the disciple. I am ready to serve you, to fight for you, to die for you. But what you are asking of me now is impossible."

I have found over the years that when I suggest to a group of people that they might take off their shoes as a preparation for meditation, some object strongly; often they say, "it will show the holes in my socks", but those holes in their socks signify a much deeper fear which is focused in the protest of Peter *"You shall never wash my feet"*. You are asking me not just to expose my naked feet but to open my whole self to you, to peel off the protective layers behind which I hide and to make myself vulnerable, to stop pretending and to recognize my own deep needs, my weakness, my clumsiness, and above all my fear that I am not loveable. Then you are asking me to let you wash my feet; I must receive the outpouring of your personality which will swamp me. I am not loveable, and you are asking me to accept your love, and this is impossible. *"You shall certainly not wash my feet for eternity"* – literally the words mean "you shall not wash my feet into the new age". In this moment, when your hour has come, you shall not "love me into the end".

If Peter cannot enter into his own weakness and vulnerability then he cannot receive the free gift. *"If I do not wash you"*, says Jesus, *"you have no part with me"*. I am not proposing to swamp you with my own overwhelming personality, but to set free the truth in you so that you may become my partner. *"Then not my feet only"*, Peter exclaims, *"but also my hands and my head"*. Jesus replies, *"The one who has bathed only needs to wash his feet, and then he is altogether clean"*.

A young father told me how he had come to a fresh

understanding of this verse. He and his little son had been playing on the beach together, and when it was time to go home the boy was covered with sand. He ran down to the sea and splashed himself clean in the water, but as he came back up the beach his feet were covered with sand again, so his father had to pick him up and wash his feet and dry them with a towel. As he did this he remembered "This is what my father used to do to me when I was a boy" – this is what fathers do, they wash their sons' feet, and those sons wash the feet of their sons, and so on ad infinitum.

So Jesus was doing for his disciples what his Father had done for him. Now they must do it for each other. *"If you know these things, happy are you if you do them."* The happiness he speaks of here is the happiness in the heart of God, which they will experience as they do what God does. It is the happiness of sharing his glory which is the dance of love, but this glory can only be entered through suffering as Jesus will make even clearer in the next movement of the dance. In his suffering they must recognize the glory – *"I tell you now before it happens so that when it happens you will believe that I AM"*. Then I shall send you out to suffer and to love as my representatives; the pattern will unfold from the Father to me and from me to you. *"He who receives you receives me, and he who receives me receives my Father who sent me."*

THE THIRD MOVEMENT: THE DANCE OF LOVE BETWEEN THE FRIENDS OF JESUS JOHN 13 [21-35]

Now the relation between Jesus and his friends is to be reflected in their relations with each other; he commands them to follow this example – to enter into glory through their own weakness.

What he commands is impossible, and with the best will in the world they cannot achieve it, because their very will, or psyche, which is commanded to make this response is locked into a psychological concentration camp of corporate evil from which they cannot escape by their own contriving. He must himself enter that realm of corporate evil, which as we all discover to our deep dismay is the shadow side of corporate love, and he must provide the way out; only then will his command become credible.

So we read "*Jesus was thrown into confusion in his spirit*"; no longer in his psyche, but in that spiritual centre of his being where human nature meets God and where heaven and earth can become one. He says "*Amen! Amen! I tell you, one of you will betray me*", or literally "will hand me over". One of those companions sitting round the supper table, who should be growing with him into mutual vulnerability, will treat him as an object to be handed over to the secular power. St John does not record at this point the breaking of the bread, which we remember at the Eucharist: "On the same night that he was betrayed he took bread, and gave thanks, and broke it and gave it to his disciples". He records another act in which Jesus gives, to Judas only, one small piece of bread dipped in the bitter sauce which was in the dish surrounding the Passover lamb. Then he tells us "*with the bread Satan entered into Judas*" – Satan who is the "prince of this world" and the ruler of darkness. Here is the rejection of love. Jesus is about to be dipped or plunged into the darkness of corporate evil. The Greek word for dip is *baptein*, which means to plunge into the depths, and comes from the same root as *baptizein*, to baptise. Jesus is being plunged into the very opposite of glory, for if glory is the interplay of love, Judas has become the agent of its polar opposite, and where there should be glory between Jesus and his friend there is separation and darkness. We read that Judas, "*having received the bread, immediately went out; and it was night*".

But Jesus, being plunged into the darkness of evil, is in the very same moment being baptised into the deepest depths of glory; for now, as at his baptism in the River Jordan, the heavens are opened; and a voice says again in his heart "thou art my beloved Son" and he knows himself to be the ladder not only between earth and heaven but between the realm of Satan and the Father's house. *When Judas had gone out, Jesus said "Now is the son of man glorified"*; now through the rejection of love the Son is revealing the glory of the Father. My children, you are to be with me in that glory, but for a little while I have to leave you, because *"where I am going you cannot come"*. The meaning of those words will be revealed to us in the following movements of the dance. Meanwhile, Jesus says *"I give you a new commandment"*.

> Love one another
> as I have loved you
> that you too should love one another

It has to be a commandment, for we could never do it out of our own volition. I remember a retired army officer, one of the military knights of Windsor who lived in a grace and favour house within the precincts of the castle. Every year the Queen used to give a party for these loyal old knights, and this particular officer who had grown very old indeed was finding it difficult to stand in the presence of his sovereign. She invited him to sit down, but he replied, "I cannot sit in your presence, ma'am". "It's an order", she said. So he sat down with great relief, but also with delight, because he had received a direct order from his supreme commander.

So Jesus gives a commandment to his disciples to do what they most want to do, yet most fear to do. It has to be a commandment because they cannot do it by any effort of their own ego, but only by letting go the ego in obedience to a direct order from their supreme commander. The first clause of the command, "Love one another as I have loved

111

you" orders them to become empty, putting their ego-selves
into God's hands for each other. The second clause, "I have
loved you in order that you should love one another" means
that I have opened the way for you to do what would be
otherwise impossible.

THE FOURTH MOVEMENT: THE DANCE OF LOVE WITHIN
THE SOUL JOHN $13^{36}-15^{17}$

"Lord, where are you going?" asked Peter. *"Where I am
going you are not able to follow me now"*, Jesus replied,
*"but you will follow me later". "Lord, why am I not able to
follow you right now?"* asked Peter. Then he uses the very
words in which Jesus has described the perfection of human
love. *"I will put my psyche for you"*, he says: I will abandon
my ego-self for you. Jesus must have been moved to hear his
disciple quoting his own words back to him; but though
Peter has learnt his teacher's language he cannot yet follow
his teacher's example, and do what those words signify.
"Will you abandon your ego-self for me?" Jesus asks him.
"Before the cock crows you will deny me three times." (13^{38})
   Then he tells Peter and the other disciples how he will
make it possible for them to follow him. *"I am going to my
Father"*, he says (14^{12}). *"There are many rooms in my
Father's house, and I am going to prepare a room for you".*
(14^2) Then I will come back and lead you into that room,
and into the Father's house where I myself am living, *"so
that where I am, you may be".* (14^3)
   Where is this room? The room of which Jesus speaks is
deep inside our human nature – the secret room at the centre
of every human personality. As we have already seen, in the
religious tradition of India it is known as the cave of the
heart, that empty place in which we can meet God. In St
John's gospel it is called the *koilia*, which means literally
the hollow space, and is used both of the womb and the

belly, the womb out of which your true self must be "born from water and spirit" – from an intercourse between human nature and God's love, and the belly out of which springs the fountain of living water which is the Spirit of God. This empty room is created in us by God, and it has the twofold and mysterious potential that it can be both within us, and at the same time in heaven. It is the place where flesh and spirit meet, the space in which the marriage of heaven and earth is consummated. It is "the still point where the dance is", the emptiness at the heart of us into which the glory of God can enter and out of which the glory of God can flow. Into that room nobody and nothing can enter except God and one's self – and not even one's ego-self, but only that ego transformed so that it is no longer I but I AM.

Jesus asks his disciples, have you not seen in the long time we have been together, that I myself am such a room – *"that I am in the Father and the Father in me?"*, and can you not believe that out of my belly is springing the fountain of his love, *"for he dwells in me doing his own works"*. (14^{10})

Now I am going to the Father's house to prepare such a room for each of you, or such a space within each of you. This is somewhere I am able to go, but where you, Peter and my other disciples, are not yet able to follow me. I can go to the Father because I am already in the Father, and the Father in me. I am a room in his house. You are not yet rooms in my Father's house. The doors of those rooms inside you are locked, but I am going to open them and invite you to come in.

Knowing that it is only an image which we shall have later to abandon, let us imagine the Father's house after the pattern of ancient Mediterranean houses to be built around an inner garden or courtyard. There are many rooms opening into this garden, and the only way we can get into the Father's house is through that particular room which he has created in the heart of each one of us. The room has two doors, one leading into our own house or apartment, and the other into the Father's garden. The door leading into our own house opens into our ego-self and the world in which we live; it is the door through which we have to enter the inner room, but it is locked on the inside. The other door leading into the garden opens into the Father's house and is kept unlocked, since there are no burglars in heaven, and is the door through which God comes into the room to meet us.

Jesus is going to the Father, and he will enter the Father's house through the room at the centre of himself; once he is in the garden he can come into our room and unlock, from inside, the door which leads into our ego-self. He has promised that if we knock, he will certainly open the door, *"Knock and it shall be opened to you"*. How this unlocking is accomplished we shall see in subsequent movements of the dance.

Having unlocked the door he calls us by our own name, and he says "Leave your ego-self behind, and come into this room in the Father's house, *'so that where I am you may be also'*. Where he is, two others will be with him. First, the Spirit. *'I will ask my Father and he will give you the Paraclete, the Spirit of Truth, so that he may live with you in this room, and in eternity"*; (v 16); the word Paraclete means literally the one who comes in answer to your cry, so that it is in response to your deepest need that the Spirit will come; and the Spirit of Truth means literally the Spirit of Reality, so that it is the Reality of God, God's glory, which will come into your deepest need. Then Jesus says something even more astonishing. *"Because you have loved me, my Father will love you, and the Father and I together will come to stay in this room with you."* As he says these things, joy breaks through and springs up inside us.

Then Jesus passes beyond the metaphor of rooms in a house and leads us into an organic metaphor of growth. It is

THE FATHER'S HOUSE

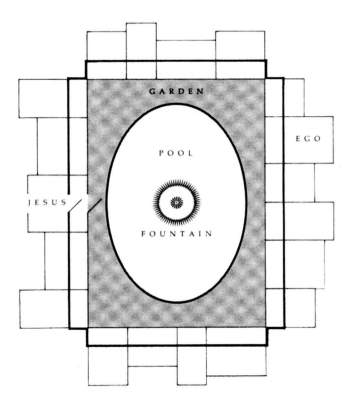

as though he is leading us out of the house and into the garden. *"I AM the true vine"*, he says, *"and my Father is the gardener"* (15¹). The vine and the gardener are dependent on each other, because the vine cannot produce good grapes without the gardener, and equally the gardener cannot make wine without those good grapes. Then he continues *"I AM the vine, and you are the branches"* (v 5); you and I are also dependent on each other, for the vine can do nothing without its branches, and the branches can do nothing without the vine. *"Dwell in me, and I in you."* He amplifies and explains this; *"Let my words (my commands) dwell in you"* (v 7), and flow through your obedience like sap through the branches of the vine, and at the same time *"dwell in my love"* (v 9) as the branch dwells in the stock and the root system of the vine. My love is the love between the Father and myself, and that love will bear its fruit of glory in you as certainly as the vine bears grapes. Then *"your joy will be full"* (v 11). The Spirit will be in you, giving you the freedom and the ability to do what you most desire to do – *"to love one another as I have loved you"* (v 12).

Then it is as though the Father himself is saying to each of us "My beloved Son, my beloved daughter, you were dead and you are alive again. You were lost and you are found. Now come out into the garden, and meet all the others who have entered into their Father's house, each through their own inner room. There you will find everybody who ever has or ever will accept our invitation to the marriage feast of heaven and earth; they are clean and shining in their wedding garments, and they have been given to each other. There in eternity you will find everything which has ever been created, the rocks, the trees, the animals, the laws of physics and psychology; they have been transformed around the centre of Jesus into a new creation, and they all cry together 'Jesus Christ is Lord: he has revealed to us the glory of the Father.'"

THE FIFTH MOVEMENT: THE SPIRIT IS THE DANCE
JOHN 15^{18} – 16^{33}

In receiving the Spirit the disciples are being given to each other, and now the dance will unfold through their life together.

The pattern of the dance will be that archetypal pattern which they have seen in Jesus. The glory of God will reveal itself as the marriage of heaven and earth, and it will flow through their emptiness; inevitably, therefore, this glory must come through suffering.

"*The world will hate you*", says Jesus (15^{19}), and by the world he means the world-order of human ego-centricity and power-politics. It will hate you because, first, you will not conform to it; you will challenge it to change, by presenting to it the vision of another social order in which each person is of absolute value, and all belong together in an organic interdependence. The world-order which will hate you is based on different values to these. So it was then in the time of Jesus, and so it is now in our own generation, and the difference is illustrated by two stories I have heard recently from people working in the City of London. One of them was employed in a merchant bank, and having received a pay rise she wished to pass it on to charity; she was sent for by the managing director and warned that such behaviour was not in accord with the ethos of the bank. The other, who was a manager in a business with many employees, suggested that the success of the business might be enhanced if they paid more regard to the people who worked for them; he was told that if he began putting people before excellence there was no place for him in the company. These two stories are almost unbelievable, but they represent an age-old trend within the world-order that the rich, as they get more secure in their riches, become less sensitive to the truth of their own human nature.

The second reason why the world will hate you, says

117

Jesus, is because you will strip away their pretences and show up their sin (v 22) – that is to say, how far they fall short of glory. For these two reasons the Spirit within you, interacting with the powers of this world, will indeed lead you into a dance of love – but it will be a dance in which love is rejected.

In this rejection of love the Spirit will be *"bearing witness"* to Jesus (v 26) – the Greek word is *martyrein*, which means literally to bear witness or give evidence, and from which comes our English word martyr, one who bears witness by suffering for the truth's sake. The Spirit, and the disciples in whom the Spirit lives, will bear witness to the truth in Jesus by suffering as he did. They will be rejected by the world in general, and most particularly by that part of the world order which is called the religious establishment – *"they will excommunicate you, and whoever kills you will think that he is doing God a service"* 16[2]) – for in religious establishments and religious fundamentalism, then as now, there can be found the most deadly focus of ego-centricity and power-politics, the fiercest resistance to change, and the most deeply engrained self-deception masquerading under the guise of spirituality.

Through their suffering the disciples will reveal new facets of glory, and Jesus tells us something deeply disturbing about the nature of that emptiness out of which such a revelation will come. *"It is expedient for you that I go away. For if I do not go away the Paraclete will not come to you"* (v 7). In order to receive the Spirit it is necessary that the disciples let go Jesus, their founder and teacher. Out of the pain of the absence of Jesus they will receive the Paraclete, coming in answer the their cry.

When he comes, he who is the Spirit of Truth, he will refute the presuppositions on which the world-order operates, and on which religious fundamentalism is based. He will show the world that justice cannot be achieved through a legal system alone, but through recognizing also

118

the unique value and potential in each person – for he himself, the Spirit of Reality, is the dance between the community and the person. He will show the religious fundamentalists that God cannot be defined once and for all in any formula, or contained within any system of thought, because he the Spirit of Reality is the dance between the old and the new, between eternity and time, between the tradition of our ancestors and our own rediscovery of their truth in the new context of today.

"*I have still many things to say to you*", he tells them, "*but you cannot bear them now. However when he comes, who is the Spirit of Truth, he will lead you into the whole truth*" (vv 12-13). The Spirit will not "*speak out of himself*" as though he was saying something basically new, but he will "*take what is mine and reveal it to you*" explaining it gradually, as you and he walk together (v 14). For this learning to proceed it is necessary that I, your teacher, go away; you will see me no more with your physical eyes but you will meet me again and see me face to face in my Father's house, there, in that secret room inside yourselves, where God and human nature meet. There the Spirit will come and reveal to you and share with you another aspect of my glory, for he will be my prayer springing up out of your own heart, and as that prayer flows through you, you will yourselves be dancing the dance of love. In my name – as my representatives – you will ask the Father directly for what you want (v 23), and the Father will give you in my name what you ask for, "*so that your joy may be full*" (v 24).

What they will ask for in his name, and receive in his name, is glory. This will become clear in the next movement of the dance, as Jesus himself asks the Father for what it is that he really wants. For now the hour is coming when he will speak no longer in metaphors, but will proclaim to them openly the reality towards which all the metaphors have been pointing (v 25). That reality is the Father.

The hour is coming when even the little company of his friends will be scattered and he will be left alone. But "*I am not alone because the Father is with me*" (v 32). The glory which will meet him in that aloneness lies deeper than any human camaraderie or spiritual euphoria, which we often mistake for glory; it is the dance of love between the aloneness of the Son and the aloneness of the Father, as they weep together and suffer together, as by their compassion they overcome the world-order of evil, and set free the joy which is at the heart of creation.

THE SIXTH MOVEMENT: THE LORD'S PRAYER IS THE DANCING John 17

After this conversation with his disciples Jesus goes where we cannot follow him. "You cannot follow me now", he had said to Peter, "but you will be able to follow me later". He is going to the Father's house.

He is no longer talking in metaphors about the Father, but going to meet the Father in that secret room within himself which is at the same time in heaven.

He is no longer talking about glory, but the Father is coming to welcome him home into the glory which is prior to the foundation of the universe. He is no longer talking about love, but as he prays, his prayer is the dance of love between heaven and earth.

We cannot grasp this prayer with our human minds. I, the writer, cannot describe it, and you, the reader, cannot understand it. We cannot see the dance until we too are in the Father's house, any more than I could see the Greek folk-dancing in Santorini until I was sitting in the *taverna*; and we cannot understand the dance until we join in the dancing. Our problem is that we are not able to go where Jesus has gone; the door through ourselves and into the Father's house is locked, and we can only knock and wait, and cry out in longing. In the final movements of the dance we shall see how Jesus opens the gate of glory by giving us to each other. Then we may begin to know within ourselves the pattern of the dance as we join in the dancing, and to understand his prayer as it prays itself through us – for the Lord's prayer is the dancing.

Jesus *"lifted his eyes to heaven"* (v 1). Now he has entered his own inner room, and his Father's house. He prays *"Father, the hour has come. Glorify your son, so that your son may glorify you."* He prays for glory. Confronted by death he prays for what he really wants, and for what you and I and every human person really wants. He prays to be loved by the Father and to love the Father, for this is the glory of God in heaven, and it is reflected on earth in the covenants we make with each other on our wedding day. "I John take you Mary ... I Mary take you John ... to love and to cherish till death us do part." We desire in the core and centre of our being to be loved and to love, both in time till death takes away our lover, and also in the eternal depths of each present moment with a timeless love which cannot die. This is how we potentially are, and what we were created to be. For this ultimate joy Jesus prays, both for himself and for his disciples.

His prayer for glory had already been answered in time, for as he prayed for glory the Father had given him the disciples. This may seem a surprising answer to his prayer, until we reflect that the glory of any great teacher is not that he should be honoured with doctorates from many universities, but that his truth should come alive in his pupils. *"Glorify your son, so that your son may glorify you."* Through the disciples the Father will give glory to Jesus, and Jesus will give that glory back to the Father, as the disciples come to know the Father in the dance of love, and as they reveal his glory to the world.

But this glory in time issues from an eternal glory. The Father has given to Jesus authority to transform the whole of human nature, and the Greek word for authority is *exousia*, which means literally "out of being" (*ex* = out of: *ousia* = being). This authority springs out of the being of the Godhead, because it arises out of the communion of love between the Son and the Father, which is *"prior to the foundation of the world"* (v 5). It is the eternal truth at the heart of the universe. It is the stuff and the energy out of which the universe is made, and it is reflected in everything that has been created. The dance of love is the heart beat that pulses through the whole body of the universe.

So Jesus prays for the disciples that the eternal glory may be in them, on earth as it is in heaven, *"that they may be one, just as we are one"* (v 11).

As he prays this prayer he is not asking the Father for something as though he needed to change the Father's mind. It is a prayer of asking, but not of asking *for* anything. It is a prayer of asking questions. The Greek word is *eroto*: I ask a question. The proper dialogue between his human nature and God is that he should ask the Father questions and that the Father should answer them, so that he may receive what the Father gives and do what the Father says.

The agonizing question which Jesus now asks the Father is "how can glory co-exist with evil?" If the Lord's prayer is flowing through us, then we are asking this question with him, and listening for the Father's answer. A Jew, Elie Wiesel, who survived the horror of Auschwitz, into which he was sent as a boy of 14, has spoken of his sense that there are two parallel universes, in one of which God reigns, and in the other of which God does not reign. Could this be the beginning of an answer, coming out of the heart of the agony itself? The first universe is the order of eternal reality or truth. The second universe is an order of hideous and banal unreality; it is the world-order of our personal ego-centricity compounded by our corporate systems of power politics, which accumulates within itself and gives birth to a monstrous reality of evil. Within that order God's laws do not operate. Now the hour has come for Jesus to enter that hideous unreality of evil, to suffer there, and to die there. The hour has come for the Father to look into that abyss of unreality and to see and to suffer with his Son; the Father will see evil through him, for he is the apple of God's eye, and suffer with him the despair of that dark night where human nature is separated from God.

Jesus prays for his disciples *"I do not ask you questions about taking them out of the world, but about keeping them from evil"* (v 15). The Greek word which we translate as keeping is *terein*, which means to keep looking at, or to hold in mind. Jesus asks, "Will you remember them in the midst of evil?" and the answer comes "I will hold them in my mind, and be there with them, suffering with them". In face of that evil and suffering God can only weep. But it is in that place where the Father and the Son weep together with the disciples whom they love that they will give those disciples glory, by giving them to each other, "so that they may be one as we are one".

In the assurance of that promise Jesus prays *"consecrate them in the truth"* (v 17). The Greek word for reality or truth, is *aletheia*, which means literally that which cannot be forgotten (*a* = not: *lethe* = forgetfulness). The prayer is both a question and an answer. "How will you hold them in glory in the midst of evil?", and the answer comes "I will hold them in the truth (*aletheia*)". Reality will not forget them in the midst of unreality.

"Your word is truth", says Jesus to the Father (v 17). Your word is the reality which created the whole universe, and your promise can never be forgotten.

"You are my word", the Father replies. I am sending you as my reality into the midst of unreality. I have not forgotten them in that God-forsaken darkness, and through your compassion you will set free my glory in them.

"For their sakes", Jesus says to the Father, *"I consecrate*

myself" (v 19). I put my ego-self into your hands for them, "*so that they may be consecrated in the truth*".

By setting out the prayer in this dialogue form I am presenting it as a conversation between the Father and the Son, taking place in the heart of Jesus. In the third and final part of the prayer he asks the Father a question and receives an answer about all who will hear and receive his Word down the centuries.

The question and the answer is about the promise of *agape*, "*that they may all be one, just as you Father are in me and I in you*" (v 21). "Just as you Father are in me" – because this is the deepest meaning of agape that you have let go your authority and put it into my hands – "and just as I am in you" – in that deepest sense of *agape* that I have put my psyche into your hands for other people – so may all the disciples down the ages be one. May they give authority to each other, setting free in each other what arises out of the true being of each one, and may they respect each other and respond to each other, and put their ego-selves into your hands for each other, in the dance of *agape*.

This is "*your glory which you gave to me and which I have given them, that they may be one just as we are one*" (v 22).

This will be the perfection of the glory which is already latent within them, "*that they may arrive at the goal for which they were created by becoming one*" (v 23).

Then "*the world-order will come to know that you have sent me*" (v 23). Recognizing your love in them, they will come to recognize your love in me.

We who live in a post – Auschwitz world have to ask ourselves, does this prayer penetrate into the reality and unreality of the concentration camps? Can we offer it to our brothers and sisters the Jews, knowing that Christians are in large part responsible for the horror of the holocaust? Or does it seem to rub salt into their wounds, presenting them with a perfectionist dream and a triumphalist Messiah, in whose name we have hated and persecuted them for 1900 years and finally attempted to annihilate them from the face of the earth like vermin? We have to approach them in a deep humility, knowing that what Jesus prayed for has by and large not happened on the plane of human history.

A Rabbi once said to me, "Christianity is so beautiful! If only it were true!"

May it be that there is still some climax towards which the prayer is leading us? Perhaps Jews will have to help Christians to see that truth, and to enter into that glory.

The final words of the prayer suggest that there is still some such climax, beyond the prayer itself. The Father is sending his son to show that Christianity is not only beautiful but that it can also be true; he is giving him authority to make possible the impossible commandment that the disciples should love each other as he has loved them. "*Righteous Father* (you who set right what is wrong), *the world-order does not know you* (and indeed cannot know you). *But I know you* (v 24) . . . *and to these disciples I have made known your name* (v 25); I have revealed to them your character, and the communion of love which is your glory. Now through my death I will set them free *to know that love in themselves* (v 26). I will no longer be their teacher, "*I will be in them*'" (v 26).

The hour has come. For their sake I put my life into your hands.

THE SEVENTH MOVEMENT: THE DANCE OF LOVE BETWEEN MARY AND JOHN John 19 [23-37]

Jesus, dying on the cross, gives his mother to the disciple whom he loved, and the disciple whom he loved to his mother. This is the end, or goal, towards which St John's story has been leading us. It appears at first sight to be very different from the end described in the other gospels.

In the gospels of Mark and Matthew the final words of Jesus are a cry in the darkness "My God, my God, why have you forsaken me?". John has described the agony of Jesus earlier in his story, and it is an essential element in the truth which he is revealing to us. It was expedient for Jesus that the Father should go away and leave him. It was necessary, for his work to be completed, that he should be sent into that darkness where God is not, where the image of Abba Father is broken, and where he has to let go God.

In the gospel of Luke, as he is being nailed to the cross and as he hangs on the cross, Jesus speaks words of forgiveness; for the soldiers, "Father forgive them", and for the terrorist crucified beside him, "today you shall be with me in Paradise". This again is an essential element in the truth which John is revealing; the work of Jesus, as we shall see in the last movement of the dance, can be summed up as forgiveness, or letting go and setting free.

John weaves together these two elements into a single truth. Jesus has to let go God – in order that he may give freedom to us. He has to stop clinging to any image of God, for then the Holy Spirit can flow out of his emptiness, and the love of God through his compassion. Then he can say to us with an authority which springs out of his own being, "Stop clinging to your images of God, and stop clinging even to me. It is expedient for you that I go away, so that you may stand up on your own feet, look at one another, respect each other, see God's reality in each other, and set free God's authority in each other. I command you to love one another, and now I am making possible what I have commanded."

When Elie Weisel was in Auschwitz he had to witness the hanging of a young boy. "We saw three gallows rearing up in the assembly place, three black crows ... Three victims in chains ... All eyes were on the child. He was lividly pale, almost calm, biting his lips ... 'Where is God? Where is He?' someone behind me asked. At a sign from the head of the camp, the three chairs tipped over ... Then the march past began. The two adults were no longer alive. Their tongues hung swollen, blue tinged. But the third rope was still moving; being so light, the child was still alive ... For more than half an hour he stayed there, struggling between life and death dying in slow agony under our eyes. And we had to look him full in the face. He was still alive when I passed in front of him. His tongue was still red, his eyes were not yet glazed. Behind me, I heard the same man asking 'Where is God now?'. And I heard a voice within me answer him 'Where is He? Here He is – He is hanging here on this gallows' ... " (E. Wiesel: *Night* (Penguin))

Elie Weisel describes how later, on the eve of Rosh Hashanah (New Year's day), the Jews in the concentration camp met to worship God. "'What are you, my God', I thought angrily, 'compared to this afflicted crowd? ... What does your greatness mean, Lord of the Universe, in the face of all this weakness, this decomposition, and this decay?' ... This day I had ceased to plead. I was no longer capable of lamentation. On the contrary I felt very strong. I was the accuser, God the accused. My eyes were open and I was alone – terribly alone in a world without God and without man. Without love or mercy. I had ceased to be anything but ashes, yet I felt myself to be stronger than the Almighty, to whom my life had been tied for so long ... I ran off to look for my father. He was standing near the wall, bowed down, his shoulders sagging as though beneath a heavy burden. I went up to him, took his hand, and kissed it. A tear fell upon it. Whose was that tear? Mine? His? I said nothing. Nor did he. We had never understood one another so clearly."

Forty-one years later Elie Wiesel became the winner of the Nobel Peace Prize. Can his experience help us Christians to understand the death of Jesus – to enter into that darkness where God is not, where God suffers and where he sets free his authority in human beings who are no longer tied to him? Can Elie, and John "the disciple whom Jesus loved", speak to each other as brothers across the centuries?

The gospel of John describes three crosses at Golgotha. On the middle cross is Jesus. At the foot of his cross, on one side, the soldiers are *dividing his clothes into four parts, to each soldier a part* (v 23). They come upon his tunic, the garment worn next to the skin, and discover that it is *not sewn together* out of different strips of material, *but woven from above through the whole.* So they say "*let us not tear it, but cast lots whose it shall be*". Why is John, at this horrific moment, going into such details about a tunic? Two Greek words provide the clue.

First, the tunic is woven from above (*anothen*). It is the same word that Jesus had used earlier in his conversation with Nicodemus when he said to him "you must be born from above", from the order of Reality where God reigns as king. This tunic woven from above, with all its vertical warps and horizontal wefts is reflecting the order in which God's love and human nature are woven together in one.

Secondly, the soldiers decide not to tear it; the Greek word is *schizomen*, from which come our English word schism – "let there be no schism", they say, "in this tunic woven from above".

The construction of the Greek sentence suggests to us that if we look on the other side of the cross we shall see what this tunic signifies.

Mary, the mother of Jesus, is standing there with her sister, and with Mary the wife of Cleopas who was said by the tradition to be the brother of Joseph the Carpenter. These three represent the human family of Jesus. Together with them were Mary of Magdala out of whom, we are told, Jesus had cast seven devils, and "the disciple whom Jesus

loved". These two represent his new spiritual family. Now
these two families are to be woven together from above, in
such a way that there will be no schism.

*Jesus says to his mother, "Woman, look! Your son!" Then
he says to the disciple, "Look! Your mother!"*

These are the two people who have been most intimately
bound up with his life, and who are now suffering most
deeply with him. The mother who loved him and gave him
birth. The disciple whom he loved and to whom he had
given a new birth. Jesus, Mary and John are together in the
darkness, broken by the power of evil, needing each other,
utterly vulnerable. All pretences are stripped away between
them. Jesus says to his mother "Let me go. See me in John.
Love him as your son". To the disciple he says "Let me go.
Be a son to my mother. Let her love you and give you birth".

From that hour, writes John, *the disciple received her
into his home* (v 27). But the Greek word he uses means
literally "into his privacy"; he received her into the secret
cave of his heart – into that hollow space which can be
translated the belly or the womb, where they are now free to
meet each other, to be for each other the Truth which was in
Jesus and to give birth in each other to his glory. For Jesus
has unlocked the door into the Father's house. It was locked
by fear, and he has opened it by compassion. He has
descended into hell, where evil reigns, and love is rejected.
Now Mary and John can recognize that ultimate darkness
within themselves, and because he is there with them and
they can face it together.

After this Jesus knew that all things were now accomplished, or we might translate "had come to their appointed
end *(telos)*". This is the same word that John had used at the
beginning of his passion story to show us the meaning of
the death of Jesus, that "having loved his own who were in
the world he loved them into the end". It is the end for
which he had prayed, "that they may be one, just as we are
one". It is the impossible new commandment being made

possible, "love one another as I have loved you, that you too should love one another".

In this end there is a beginning, for in Mary and John at Golgotha a new age is being born – a community whose destiny is to be like that tunic worn next the skin, "not stitched together but woven from above through the whole". It is to be a community of human persons across the world and down the centuries, each one unique, but responsible to one another, interdependent, and living together without a schism. In such a community the eternal glory of God will be reflected on earth as it is in heaven.

The Christian church has not looked like that, in its outward appearance. How can we respond to the Rabbi who said "Christianity is so beautiful. If only it were true!"?

I believe that we have to ask him to come and help us, because it is only together that we can discover the truth of what we have come to call Christianity. As we return to that moment at Golgotha, we recognize that it is not just two individuals who are being woven together but two spiritual families. Mary the mother of Jesus represents Judaism, which has given birth to Jesus, and fed him, and led him into the knowledge of God. The disciple whom Jesus loved represents Christianity – for in that title "whom Jesus loved" is revealed the essence of being a Christian. Jesus says to Judaism, "Look at Christianity and see your son", and to Christianity he says, "Look at Judaism and see your mother". In him these two spiritual families are not stitched together, they are woven into one from above. He is a passionately loyal Jew, and he says, "Do not change one syllable of the Torah; the God of Abraham and Isaac and Jacob has sent me to call his people back to that eternal truth which is prior to all our sacred history and hidden within each particular moment of it – before Abraham came to be, 'I AM'."

That claim flows out of his emptiness, and not out of the

imperialism of Christians who will come after him. As Jews and Christians stand together at Golgotha and in Auschwitz, in the darkness where God is not, as we share our brokenness and weep together, Jesus says to both Judaism and Christianity "let there be no schism between you or you will both be mutilated, and the wholeness which is in me will be torn apart. Be together what I AM."

After this, John writes, *in order that scripture should be accomplished*, and come to its appointed end (*telos*), *Jesus said, I thirst*. In this tiny passage of his gospel, as he records the death of Jesus, he quotes four times from the Jewish scriptures; for these scriptures are not to be superseded but fulfilled – in the glory of God which flows out of suffering. Then Jesus said, *It is accomplished* (again the word *telos*), *and bowing his head he handed over the Spirit*.

That Spirit is the to and fro of love between God and human nature, and this is the end, that Jesus should hand over the eternal truth which was in himself to Mary and John, and through them to all who in a wonderful variety of ways are giving birth to that truth in particular moments of history, or who are seeking to know it and to receive it into themselves. Especially he hands over that spirit and that truth to Judaism and Christianity. "Let me go", he says to them, "and look at one another. Respect each other. Set free the authority of God in each other. The glory of God is not contained in your exclusive religious systems, but it will be seen in the dance of love between you. Let me go, and be the Messiah/Christ together, sent by the one true God to show the human race the way through suffering into glory, and to guide them through letting go into freedom, joy and peace".

The Dance of Love

THE EIGHTH MOVEMENT: THE DANCE OF LOVE BETWEEN
HEAVEN AND EARTH JOHN 20 [1-23]

Easter day is our wedding day. *On the first day of the week,*
writes John, *comes Mary Magdalene to the tomb early while
it is still dark.* All the four gospels note that it was "the first
day of the week", and John emphasises it by repeating it
twice (v 1 and v 19). The first day of the week in the Jewish
scriptures was the beginning of creation; "in the beginning
God created the heavens and the earth". Easter day is the
beginning of a new creation; as Jesus is raised up "from
among the corpses" and ascends into heaven we see a new
heaven, and as he meets Mary Magdalene at dawn in the
garden we see a new earth; his resurrection is the marriage
of this new heaven and this new earth, in a dance of love
between the creator and the universe which he has created.

I have already, in the first part of this book (page 43),
outlined the Easter story as recorded by John, and made a
preliminary reconnoitre into the meaning of the word resurrection. We have to approach the resurrection of Jesus with
our minds, but in the end we can only know it in our hearts.
We have to approach it through suffering, but in the end we
can only know it through thanksgiving.

Archbishop Michael Ramsey once said, "There are two
ways to God – through suffering and through thanksgiving".
I want to suggest that these are not alternative ways but that
we have necessarily to go through both doors, because they
are the two doors in the cave of the heart through which we
enter the Father's house. The first door leads out of our egocentric self and into the secret room. We have to knock upon
it with our intellect and hammer upon it with our longing
and our desire. "Knock, and it shall be opened", we have
been told, and through suffering we find one day that this
door has been opened by compassion, and that we are being
welcomed home into the Father's house. Then the Father
himself invites us to go through the other door and out into

132

the garden, to celebrate the marriage of heaven and earth; he invites us to put on a wedding garment, which is thanksgiving, to meet the other wedding guests, and to join with them in the dance. I can only describe the dance "enigmatically", to use St Paul's word – "Now we see through a mirror, in an enigma", he writes, "but then face to face". What I saw in a Cretan village was perhaps an enigmatic reflection of what we shall see in heaven. Jesus, the young hero of the war of liberation, leads the dance; then he steps aside, and each of the guests in turn takes the lead, and after a little while hands over to the next in line.

But this is a wedding. Where is the bride? From within the cave of the heart, and within the Father's house, we see everything in a new light. Gradually it dawns upon us that we are together the bride. We who live in time across the world and down the ages are destined to be in eternity that community "woven together, through the whole of it from above", and without a schism. Our human nature and the Love of God are to be woven together in the to and fro of glory. We are to look at each other, and to recognize that the glory of God lies hidden within everybody, and within everything that ever has been or ever will be created. The whole universe, when looked at from the Father's house, will be seen to have the same mysterious potential we have already recognized in the cave of our own hearts, which can be at the same time in us and in heaven. The whole universe is at the same time both material and spiritual. That is how God created it, expressing his own character in it as an artist expresses himself in a work of art. That is how God sees it, and how he invites us to see it with him. As George Herbert wrote,

> A man who looks on glass,
> On it may stay his eye;
> or if he pleaseth, through it pass,
> And then the heaven espy.

Are the physicists who describe a universe in which matter is at the same time energy seeing "through a mirror, in an enigma", the reality which we shall see face to face in the Father's house? Is the glory of God the very stuff of which the universe is made? Is the energy of the Spirit, who is the to and fro of love, the reality which underlies the ecology of nature, and our own sexuality and social life?

The resurrection of Jesus is only completed and comes to its appointed end when it happens also in us. At midnight on Easter Eve the Orthodox priest cries out "*Christos aneste*": Christ is risen! In the darkness of evil and of death the Father has remembered his Son. The people reply "*alethos aneste*": truly, in the reality which cannot forget and cannot be forgotten, he is risen. The resurrection has happened objectively, outside ourselves, between Jesus and the Father. But it is also happening between Jesus and his friends. He is remembering them – for whatever the Father does for him, he does for them. So that they may be reassured that he is alive in eternity and that he remembers them in time, he comes to them out of the eternal depths of particular moments. Because he is inviting them to celebrate with him the marriage of heaven and earth, he himself comes in a form which is neither simply material nor purely spiritual, but in which matter and spirit have been made one; and he comes to his friends in a consciousness which is neither simply objective nor purely subjective, but is the consciousness of I AM in the cave of their hearts, where they are at the same time on earth and in heaven.

On the morning of the first Easter day this objective and subjective reality began to dawn in the consciousness of Mary Magdalene. She had come to the tomb, which in Greek is *mnemeion*: the place of remembrance. She thought she was coming to remember Jesus, but as she wept she discovered that he had not forgotten her.

Mary!
Rabboni – my teacher!
Do not cling to me ... Go and tell my brothers and sisters "I ascend to my Father and your Father, to my God and your God."

Do not cling to me, because resurrection appearances such as this are not the final reality of my resurrection, but let me go, so that I may enter eternity and be present with you always, and come to you out of the eternal depth of each moment of time. Then the real Jesus will be coming to you in real people – for that is the reality of the new creation. It is expedient for you that I go away, or the Paraclete will not come to you, but when that Spirit of Truth comes, then my resurrection will be fulfilled in your resurrection, and the glory which God has given to me will come to its appointed end as you remember me and I remember you, in the covenant of love which is the marriage of the new earth and the new heaven.

On the evening of the first Easter day the new creation unfolds from an individual into a community. *Later on that same day, the first day of the week, writes John, the doors being locked where the disciples were for fear of the Jews* ... (v 19). Naturally the disciples were frightened. They were living under the dictatorship of an occupying power, and they feared not only the stamping out of their liberty and the crushing of their cause, but at any moment arrest, interrogation, torture and death. But why does John write "for fear of the Jews"? Basically the Greek word *Judaios* means a Judaean, an inhabitant of Judaea and of Jerusalem in contrast to other regions such as Galilee. In the gospels of Matthew, Mark and Luke the word *Judaios* appears only 17 times, 11 of which occur in the title "King of the Judaioi" used as an insult by the Romans at the crucifixion of Jesus; three times it has the local meaning of Judaea, and three times it refers to the political and religious establishment concentrated in Jerusalem. John uses the word 71 times and always, in every single case, with this last meaning. As Jesus and his little group of Galileans come up to the capital they are confronted by the government and by the religious system. These are the Judaioi, whom John sees as the enemies of Jesus. They are the local manifestation in Judaea, and at that moment of history, of a universal world order of ego-centricity and power politics compounded by religious fundamentalism. It is the most deadly combination, fiercely resistant to change, and above all to the openness and vulnerability which was evident in Jesus.

John is obviously not using the word Judaioi of the Jewish people. Such an interpretation, if one looks at the text, is ludicrous. But for 1900 years the Jewish people have seen in the gospel of John one of the sources of their persecution by the Christians, and we Christians have allowed the gospel of John to be interpreted in this grotesque way, and the hatred of the Jews to become ingrained into our religion. By so doing we have fouled up the gospel of Love, and contaminated the fountain of Love which flows out of it. We have ourselves become a world order of power politics compounded by religious fundamentalism, which has persecuted, tortured and killed those whom God has sent to challenge it. Being afraid of the darkness within ourselves, we Christians have projected it onto others and especially onto the Jews, and in consequence have become locked into our own fears. Now we need the Jews to help us open those locked doors so that we can get out – or is it perhaps that we can get in?

To return to the Easter story. "The doors were locked where the disciples were for fear ..." The doors of their house were locked for fear of the Judaioi, and the doors of their hearts for fear of each other and of what lay within themselves. *Jesus came, and stood among them, and said "Peace to you" Having said this, he showed them his hands and his side.*

He showed them in his hands the wounds made by the nails – the evidence of his suffering and of his compassion. Now the doors locked by fear are being opened by compassion, and in the their emptiness the disciples are being given to each other, like Mary and John at the foot of the cross.

He showed them in his side the gash made by the spear, out of which these flowed after his death, as John informs us with great emphasis, both water and blood – both water, the free gift of the Spirit flowing out of his belly for them, and blood, his life put into the hands of God for them in the ultimate act of agape. Now Jesus is "loving them into the end".

Then the disciples were full of joy, seeing their Lord. Journeys end in lovers' meeting, and their joy is full and overflows as they hear him speak the name of each one, and as they respond like Mary Magdalene in the garden "Rabboni, my teacher".

In that end is a beginning – for now they have seen his glory. The word John uses here for "seeing" means to see not just the surface appearance of things but their inner reality. They have seen in him the glory of God, and now they must begin to discover it in themselves, and reveal it to other people.

Jesus said to them again "Peace to you. As the Father has sent me, so I send you". The simple secret at the heart of his own life is that he is sent by the Father. It is "a simplicity costing not less than everything", as T. S. Eliot describes it, for he has put his ego-self into the Father's hands for his friends, and in the exchange of Love between them the Father has given him "authority over all flesh" – over all human nature. Now the disciples are being sent in that same costly simplicity to share that same authority.

Having said this, he breathed on them and said, "Receive Holy Spirit". It is as though the vine were saying to the branches, "Receive sap", for Holy Spirit is God flowing through the human nature of Jesus in the dance between

137

heaven and earth. To receive Holy Spirit is to receive that dance, and to receive that dance into yourself is to find yourself dancing it.

The Spirit is the dance, and the Lord's prayer is the dancing, and as the disciples receive Holy Spirit their Lord's prayer is already springing up inside them. They have seen his glory, and they know that to be loved as he is loved, and to love as he loves, is what they really want more than anything else in the world. Out of that desire springs the prayer for glory, "Father, glorify us so that we may glorify you". What is more, they know that they are now free to choose glory, as before they were not free. Because Jesus has chosen to enter into glory through suffering, and has commanded them to follow him, the way is open for them to choose what they really want. Out of that free will springs the prayer "Father, your will be done".

Now that the disciples are both desiring and willing to receive from God what they were created to be, and to become what they truly are, the risen Jesus breathes into them the gift of I AM. It is his free gift of himself, as he comes to live with them in the cave of the heart where "I" is transformed into I AM. "Do not cling to me", he says. The disciples must not try to possess this I AM, as though it was an object, or to contain it within any outward form of community or institution, for I AM is the name of God. They can receive the free gift of Holy Spirit and of I AM but they cannot cling to it, any more than they can cling to the wind, for the wind blows where it wants to blow and not where they think it ought to blow. They can receive the gift fresh every morning, so long as they are hungry and ask urgently for it, "Father give us today our daily bread"; and they can receive it together so long as they do not hide their hunger from one another, but open their needs to each other.

The essence of I AM in Jesus is "I and the Father who sent me". He has already revealed the purpose for which the

Father has sent him. It is "that they may be one as we are one". Now he reveals to them how that purpose will be realized. It is through forgiveness, which means letting go. (See page 25). This is the Father's work, for which the disciples are now being commissioned. *"If you let go people's sins, they will be free; if you cling to people's sins they will be prisoners."* The purpose for which God created the universe will be achieved by setting free prisoners. But herein lies an amazing paradox, that if you let go people's sins, *you* will be free, and if you cling to people's sins, *you* will be the prisoner. As we come to understand this, a prayer springs up each morning out of the prison of our own ego-centricity. "Forgive us our sins, as we forgive those who trespass against us", so that we may step out into the freedom of this new day.

Without any shadow of doubt, we Christians ought to ask forgiveness from the Jews. The only doubt is in their minds, because the Christian concept of forgiveness, as it is generally misunderstood, seems to Jews somewhat dubious. We would do better to talk of letting go and setting free. In both of our traditions the central story is about setting free people who were prisoners. The Jewish story is about an Exodus, through which God sets free the Israelites from their slavery in Egypt. He hears their cry, and he sends Moses, to say to the Israelites, "I AM has sent me to you", and to Pharaoh, "Let my people go". Then God's presence leads them through the Red Sea to Mt Sinai, where they receive his law, and from Mt Sinai across the desert and into a promised land "flowing with milk and honey". The Christian story is also about an Exodus, through which God reveals his glory and sets his people free – for "exodus" is the word, springing out of his own Jewish tradition, which Jesus uses as he communes with Moses and Elijah, the two great figures of Jewish faith, about his impending death and resurrection. God sends him, like Moses, to say to his people "I AM has sent me to you", and to the ruler of this world, "Let my people go." God leads him and his disciples through the waters of death and into a resurrection, where they receive his Spirit and enter into a new creation, where Jesus reigns in a Messianic age of joy and peace.

Rooted as we are in these two stories of "letting go" and "setting free", Christians and Jews have a realistic language in which they can talk to each other about forgiveness. We Christians know that we must ask the Jewish people to forgive us our sins, but that means that we must say to them "Please come and help us, for we are in prison. Set us free to be Christians, as we set you free to be Jews".

What of the Judaioi, of whom we continue to be afraid – not only those political and religious enemies of Jesus, but all who have exercised power over us unjustly, and all religious fundamentalists? We must forgive them their sins and let them go, so that we may be set free from our own lust for power, and forgiven the most deadly sin of all, the sin of spiritual pride and of putting ourselves in the place of God.

Deeper than sin, what of evil? We cannot forgive evil. We can only ask God to rescue us from it, and hope that he has not forgotten us. Then a prayer springs up out of the evil of Auschwitz and out of the darkness and unreality within ourselves, which is the cry of our ultimate weakness "Lead us not into the time of trial, but deliver us from evil". Into our powerlessness, in answer to our cry, comes the Paraclete. He is the Spirit of that Truth which does not forget, and cannot be forgotten. He is the dance of Love between earth and heaven, not only between a beautiful earth and a happy heaven, but also between the realm of Satan and our Father's house. If we cannot receive him in time and space because our suffering is too terrible, then he has power to come through locked doors, and to be present in eternity which is in the depth of all time. "I AM", he says, "the alpha and the omega, the beginning and the end, and I have the keys of death and hell". Either in time, as we receive him, or in eternity as future generations remember, or as the whole company of earth and heaven celebrates the victory of Love, the prayer of our powerlessness is transformed into self-abandonment and thanksgiving. "Deliver us from evil, for yours is the kingdom, the power, and the glory, in time and in eternity." Amen. So let it be.

Conclusion

As I am writing these words, on 15 August 1988, news is coming through of floods in the Sudan. After torrential rains the waters of the Nile are rising, and millions of people have become homeless as their houses, built of mud and sand, are being washed away. Describing this terrible catastrophe, Andrew Gimson writes in today's *Independent*, "I never before appreciated the force of the parable about the house built on the sand, and the house established on a rock" ... *The rains came down, the floods rose, the winds blew, and beat upon that house, and it collapsed, and great was its ruin.*

The parable is calling our attention to the fundamental reality, which either does exist between ourselves and our creator leading to our survival, or does not exist between ourselves and our creator leading to our ruin. It is a reality which is reflected in the ineluctable laws of nature, such as the action of water on rock or sand. This fundamental reality is a covenant between the creator and that part of his creation which has evolved into self-consciousness – that he will speak to us, and we will hear his words and do them. *Why do you keep on calling me "Lord Lord"*, Jesus asks, *and never do what I say? Everyone who comes to me and hears my words and does them ... is like a man who, in building his house, dug deep, and laid the foundations on a rock. When the floods came, the river burst upon that house, but could not shift it, because it was well built.*

In Part I of this book we listened to some of his key words, and in Part III to the Word itself, the message which comes through his spoken words; now we might conclude that the time has come to roll up our sleeves and do what he has said. Such a mood often emerges in Christian circles after a long debate, or a difficult period of restructuring. We exhort each

143

other and encourage ourselves with cries of "Forward to
mission!"; there is a light in every eye and a smile on every
face. But after a little while the light grows dimmer, and the
smile sets into a mask. Yes, we are being *sent* – that is the
meaning of the word mission. But to do what?

As we examined the key words of the Christian faith we
discovered that they are drawn together and assemble themselves round the word "glory"; and as we listened to the
Word itself, we heard once again that *the Word became flesh
and revealed his glory,* so that we saw in a human personality the glory of the Godhead. That glory is the dance of
love – the eternal dance of the Trinity in heaven which is
reflected in the creation, and in which we are invited to
join; this is the reality with which we must co-operate if our
civilization is to survive and not to collapse in ruins. For the
Word is the pattern of reality; if we do not co-operate with
it, that reality will break us, but if we do, it will set us free
to become what we are created to be.

To hear the word and do it is not to submit to a pattern of
servile obedience, but it is to enter into the dance of love –
to recognize the glory and to let it break through into what
we are and what we do. Our prototype is Mary the mother
of Jesus, whose festival day it is on August 15; with her we
are invited to receive into our womb the spirit who is this
dance of glory, to allow Reality to overshadow us, and in
self-abandonment and thanksgiving to say "Here am I, the
Lord's servant. Let it happen to me according to your
word".

Glory breaks into our emptiness, and if we try to define
it or to grasp hold of it, then it disappears. But if we return
to the prayer of Moses with which this book began, "Lord,
show me your glory", then we hear the answer which God
gave him, that he must remember. As God passes by, Moses
must hide in the cleft of a rock, because to see God's glory
face to face would be to die, but when God has passed, then
he can peep out and see God's backside.

Conclusion

So now I want to share with you, my reader, three such memories in the hope that it will encourage you to remember and to see the backside of God's glory for yourself.

1 PEOPLE AND CITIES

I remember that in 1968 we held an international conference at Coventry Cathedral called "People and Cities", to confront the problems of the modern city. Planners, politicians and church leaders from thirty-three countries accepted our invitation to meet together. As we began listening to each other, and to the insights of our opening speaker Constantine Doxiadis, the complexity of the modern city became apparent – its geography, its people, the various buildings such as houses, shops, factories and theatres, and its networks such as traffic systems, electricity and drains. He showed us that there are at least five ways of looking at a city, and so of seeing it differently through five different spectacles – through economics, politics, society, technology and culture. As we struggled during our time together to grasp this objective complexity of the city, we grew amongst ourselves, in little groups, to know each other better across the divisions of races and nations and professions. At the end of the conference there was a service of worship in the Cathedral, and within that service a moment when we sat in silence and Hephzibah Menuhin played Bach on a piano. Within that music there was a moment when, very slowly and gently, the minor key turned into the major key.

Perhaps the music said it for us. Out of our problem was appearing the answer to the problem. Out of the complexity of the city was emerging the glory of the city – for the word complexity means literally "embracing", and the glory of the city, waiting to be born, was the dance of love. The pattern of that Reality was imposing itself on our confusion. The glory of God was seeking to express itself, and to be "born again from above" through our life together and out into the cities of the world. "Love one another, as I have loved you." If you hear that word and do it, the city will be saved; if you hear that word and do not do it the city will collapse in ruins.

2 THE PHYSICAL UNIVERSE

I remember in that same year of 1968 lying on a beach in one of the Greek islands, sun-bathing, and talking with Professor C. M. Waddington, the biologist from Newcastle. He was introducing me to some of the insights of modern scientists, and from him I first heard the word ecology. It is almost incredible, now, that the word was unknown to the general public as late as 1968, but a professor of physics has since told me that he only became aware of the word in 1965, and it is not included in the Shorter Oxford English Dictionary of 1933 – so recent is the rediscovery of this insight which was common knowledge to our remote ancestors. Professor Waddington spoke also about a "necessary path" in evolution, a "chreode" as he called it, using a technical term derived from the Greek *Chree:* it is needful or necessary, and *odos:* the way. The evidence for such a "necessary path" suggested the possibility of some kind of purpose in the universe, though he himself was an agnostic on this question. As we talked, I began to sense a universe in which God and nature and my own human nature would all be at home together.

Since then I have taken every opportunity to explore this further and over the last two years a group has been meeting at the Abbey, Sutton Courtenay, to examine the interface between religion and science. We have enjoyed, on the theological side, the leadership of Fr Ted Yarnold, SJ, and on

Conclusion

the scientific side the leadership of Dr Rupert Sheldrake and Professor Brian Goodwin, who in common with many other scientists are questioning the mechanistic view of the universe which has been current since Newton published the *Principia* in 1667.

Newton's work, they explained to us, represented a "paradigm shift" from the medieval view of the universe, in which nature was seen to be alive and responding to the love of God. By contrast, Newton described a universe of dead material objects, governed by transcendent laws. He was a religious man, but a Unitarian and not a Trinitarian; his God was separated from nature, and no longer involved with his creation in the to and fro of love, but was more like a clock-maker who had made and wound up a clock, or the designer of a machine which could now operate according to its own inbuilt laws such as the law of gravity. Newton's "mechanistic synthesis" of God and nature, said Brian Goodwin, has been described as a shift from love to gravity, and the question is now being asked "are we witnessing a shift back from gravity to love?"

Rupert Sheldrake, reflecting on our discussion, wrote, "Modern physics has transformed the old-fashioned concept of matter as hard, impenetrable, dark unconscious stuff, following inexorable laws in a thoroughly predetermined manner. The nature of matter now seems to depend on vibratory patterns of energy, bound within fields of probability". He described those fields to us as demonstrating a quality of interdependence, in which each part of the field recapitulates the whole field, and the whole field reacts to the movement of each part, and the different fields are nested together and interact with each other in a complexity which the human mind cannot grasp.

As I hear what these scientists say I can only wonder, "Is the eternal glory of God, which is the dance of love, seeking to reveal itself once again to our generation reflected in our consciousness of the physical universe?" And as I listen to

147

them talking, admitting in all humility the disintegration of their former world view, and their disillusionment with the effects of their own technology which are clearly so evil as well as so good, and as I see them letting go their former prejudices and their old dogmatic orthodoxy, then I wonder to myself, "Who are really hearing the Word of God and doing it – these scientists, or the fundamentalist theologians who attack them?"

If mankind can hear that word and do it, and co-operate reverently with the Reality of how things are, then our planet may yet be saved. If we hear that word and do not do it, because it would be economically too difficult, then our environment will collapse, and we ourselves will be overwhelmed in the great catastrophe.

3 INTER-FAITH PRAYER

Last year my friend Peter Talbot-Willcox and I, who have been engaged in inter-faith discussion for twelve years, found ourselves becoming increasingly frustrated. We were endlessly talking about God and discussing God in our heads, but we were not allowing the God we were talking about to take the initiative, and make himself known to us in our hearts. So we invited one Hindu, one Moslem, one Jew and one Buddhist to join with us for twenty-four hours, and to ask "Can we pray together?" We suggested that each of us should bring a symbol of prayer from our own tradition.

We met at the Abbey in Sutton Courtenay. At supper we read St Paul's hymn to love and after supper we went to the meditation room, where we sat in a circle on the floor, round an upright wooden beam which had stood there since the fifteenth century. Each of us laid on the floor the symbol he or she had brought. The Hindu had brought a photograph of his guru; the Moslem a book of theology; the Jew a prayer shawl and a prayer book; Peter had brought a rosary from Mount Athos, and I an icon of the Trinity. The Buddhist had brought a stupa, whose shape represented the perfection of the Buddha, and with it a book which he said had helped him on his way – "The Imitation of Christ" by Thomas à Kempis. As we laid these symbols on the floor we explained their meaning. Then we sat in silence. At the end of the silence we bowed to each other and went to bed.

The next morning we asked ourselves, "What happened?" We could only say this, that five doors had been opened into the mystery of God, and that the mystery which cannot be grasped by the human mind, and who is the one true God beyond all our imaginings, had entered into the room through those five open doors and given himself to us. If we had asked "Can we pray together?" the answer would have been "No, you can't". But if we handed the responsibility over to the mystery, and allowed him or her to take his or her own initiative, then the answer became "Yes, I will come and be in you what you are seeking for".

That group met on two further occasions. Throughout our prayer and our discussions each of us was rediscovering from the others truth already present in our own tradition but which we had not recognized so clearly before. At the end, each of us went away a better Hindu, Moslem, Jew, Christian or Buddhist. We learnt that God was at home in all our forms, and therefore we must no longer be exclusive. We found that each of us, in describing prayer, said that we were "remembering the divine reality".

After the meetings our Moslem friend, Professor Hasan Askari, summed up the experience as "Presence in prayer. To be present *with* a person of another religious tradition in his or her act of prayer was something apart from and above our conceptual modes of self-understanding and of understanding the other ... To enter into the prayer of another religious tradition does not mean giving up or denying one's own religious tradition, but moving beyond it. Hence the surprise, the unexpected ease, the sense of well-being". Our

Buddhist friend Santacitto, a monk, wrote "We have begun to share something very special, something which to blossom fully must be allowed its organic growth". He added:

> There was a benediction in our silent
>   communion
> A sharing of blessing in our open-hearted
>   communication
> And in our giving of our common humanity
>   we began to taste the special grace
>   of community

"But these are clever words which tell me that I am already saying too much". Peter Talbot-Willcox wrote "Inter-faith *discussion* tends to accentuate the polarities of religions and of methods ... inter-faith *prayer* is mutual recognition of a shred and always mysterious origin of mankind and of the creation. I doubt whether it would be generally beneficial for people to use forms of vocal prayer foreign to their own tradition and practice, but perhaps better to observe periods of silence, during which each participant would be free to follow his or her own interior path, rather than attempting the ascent by two or more paths at the same time. It seems to be sensible to persevere with one's own method, although it may be useful to *observe* the methods of others."

As I remember these happenings I see the backside of the glory; that it has revealed itself in answer to our needs, both our personal needs and the apparently desperate needs of our generation, that it is the reality which is searching for us and can save us, and that it is the dance of love which we shall only know as we join in the dance.

This implies, first that we meet each other in a way which itself resembles a dance of love – listening to each other, respecting each other, and setting free the truth in each other, in small groups where the reality can break through our pretences and our prejudices. The glory is not only the truth towards which we are journeying, but it is also the way we have to travel.

It implies, secondly that we hear the words and do them. In order to hear them we have to return to the source, and rediscover their original meaning. They are like signposts which have been twisted round, so that they no longer point us towards home but towards a concentration camp, no longer towards the true God who sets us free but towards a monster god who exists only in our own sick fantasy, an almighty dictator, exclusive, holding us all together in a prison of unreality, and each one of us, so that we shall not struggle nor protest, strapped into a strait-jacket of guilt and fear. In order to hear the words we have to twist the signposts back into their original position, so that they point towards the glory represented in that icon of the Trinity reproduced inside the cover of this book. There is revealed the supreme value and the eternal truth at the heart of the whole creation – the dance of love within the very being of the Godhead.

In order to "do" the words, we have to allow that glory to break into the secret centre of our own being, and from there to overflow through what we are together, and to confront our society with a way of life which is a radical alternative to itself. Over the centuries little groups of people have done this, like St Francis and his brothers in the thirteenth century, or l'Arche in our own day, always conscious of their shortcomings but at the same time infectious with joy – as someone has said of St Francis, not knowing whether to laugh or to cry. By and large, Christendom and Christianity have failed to do this, though in every time and place "where two or three are gathered together in my name" the vine has not failed to bear fruit through its branches.

Now, as my friend Raimundo Panikkar suggests, Christendom and Christianity are emerging into a new self-under-standing which he calls Christianness. In that self-understanding the reality of Christ is no longer focused in the institutions of Christendom – in the churches and nations, the laws, the cathedrals and the inquisitions, nor in Christianity – in the credal statements of the Faith, but in the way of Christ being lived, often by young people outside the credal structures of the churches. They are drawn to this way because they recognize its self-evident truth, in contrast to their own contemporary culture.

But there is a danger of trying to do the words without hearing them. There is a drug on the market called *Ecstasy,* which is said to make people dance, to create harmony between them and to dissolve blockages within the psyche, to produce "an overwhelming feeling of peace; and a lot of insights into yourself". But a report on this drug warns of side effects, of nausea, giddiness and jaw tension, and after prolonged use, of anxiety, confusion and depression. It draws attention to the dangers of intense dancing under the influence of a drug that boosts heart rate and blood pressure.

The way of Christ, I have suggested, is a way of "ecstasy" in the sense of "standing out" beyond your ordinary mind (see page 59). But if you aim for the ecstasy of Jesus without the death of Jesus, and without his raising-up through death by the Father into the new creation, then you are in danger of falling into that spiritual pride which is the most deadly of all the deadly sins, because it is to put yourself in the place of God.

The fundamental reality is "to hear my words and do them". As you hear them and do them, the words themselves are transformed. They are no longer signs, they become symbols. As a wedding ring is not just a sign that you are married, but a symbol of your marriage, so the words are no longer just signs pointing towards God, but symbols alive with his reality, and they reverberate through the cave of your heart which is both in yourself and in your Father's house. His presence has entered into them, and they begin to have authority within themselves to confront you – and sometimes to play jokes on you.

Here are three jokes they are playing on me, as this book comes to an end, about hearing and doing. First they say to me, "Ask the fundamentalists for forgiveness. You have said that they commit the fundamental error of trying to define God in words. But look at them! Recognize also in these brothers and sisters of yours the fundamental reality, that they are committed to hearing the words and doing them. In this they are more loyal than you are. Ask them to come and help you, and to set you free to be a better Christian as you set them free to be better fundamentalists".

Secondly, the words take me back to the opening sentence of my own foreword. "Look!" they say, "you were walking with your god-daughter Zoe along the Ridgeway, and following the signs. The message of your book, which you have written with such toil and trouble, was already implicit in that opening sentence. The Ridgeway was your *chreode,* your 'necessary way'. The signs were pointing to the truth of how things are, and the name Zoe means life. The reality of I AM was already present, waiting to reveal itself. 'I AM the way *(odos),* the truth *(aletheia)* and the life *(zoe):* no one comes to the Father's house except through me' – except through following the way I AM, and doing the truth I AM, and living the life I AM. The reality you thought you were searching for was searching for you; before you wrote this book it was already reflecting itself in your walking. It is already breaking through what you and Zoe are actually doing in the present tense. So don't take yourself too seriously, or think that you have said anything new. Let your book go, so that you may be free to do ordinary things and to recognize in ordinary people how extraordinary they are."

That was the beginning of the book. Now, thirdly, as we

arrive at the end of the book, the words which are laughing
at me are the words of my wife Sandra. She said to me
yesterday, speaking out of her love for me and her exaspera-
tion with me, "Why do you create such a song and dance
about everything?" Why indeed? What am I compensating
for? In the still centre of her being she knows that we do not
create the dance, but that the dance has already created us.
She knows in her heart the truth T. S. Eliot wrote about,
that

> Except for the point, the still point
> There would be no dance, and there is
> only the dance.

By her I am drawn back into that way, which is our
"necessary way"; in her I see that truth – the reality which
can never forget or be forgotten, so that when it is forgotten
we disintegrate and cease to be; and with her at that still
point, but only at that still point, I can share the suffering
and the joy which is the dance of love, and is our own true
life together.

Lightning Source UK Ltd.
Milton Keynes UK
UKOW01f0610200217

294805UK00001B/19/P